SPIRIT
OF THE
BLUEGRASS

Strange, Surprising,
and Sentimental Stories
from Kentucky

MARVIN
BARTLETT

Globe
Pequot
Essex, Connecticut

Globe Pequot

An imprint of The Globe Pequot Publishing Group, Inc.
64 South Main Street
Essex, CT 06426
www.globepequot.com

Distributed by NATIONAL BOOK NETWORK

British Library Cataloguing in Publication Information available

Library of Congress Cataloging-in-Publication Data

Names: Bartlett, Marvin, author.
Title: Spirit of the Bluegrass : strange, surprising, and sentimental stories from Kentucky / Marvin Bartlett.
Description: Essex, Connecticut : Globe Pequot, 2025. | Summary: "Spirit of the Bluegrass takes readers to Kentucky to soak up the spirit of the people, places, and things unique to the Bluegrass State"—Provided by publisher.
Identifiers: LCCN 2024052200 (print) | LCCN 2024052201 (ebook) | ISBN 9781493086795 (paperback) | ISBN 9781493086801 (epub)
Subjects: LCSH: Kentucky—Social life and customs.
Classification: LCC F456.2 .B37 2025 (print) | LCC F456.2 (ebook) | DDC 976.9—dc23/eng/20250130
LC record available at https://lccn.loc.gov/2024052200
LC ebook record available at https://lccn.loc.gov/2024052201

∞™ The paper used in this publication meets the minimum requirements of American National Standard for Information Sciences—Permanence of Paper for Printed Library Materials, ANSI/NISO Z39.48-1992

CONTENTS

INTRODUCTION

As a lifelong television news watcher, I have always liked the last story in the newscast. It is never hard news. That is where they put the video of water-skiing squirrels and record-breaking pumpkins and the world's ugliest dog. When I was young, my family always had the *CBS Evening News with Walter Cronkite* on our TV after dinner. I became a fan of the show-closing "On the Road with Charles Kuralt" segments. I thought he had the best job in the world, as he traveled around the country in a recreational vehicle and met ordinary people with extraordinary stories.

Although I lived on a farm in north-central West Virginia, on clear days, our antenna was able to pull in a couple of stations from Pittsburgh. They also had reporters who did traveling segments, which I watched with close attention.

I decided when I was in high school that I would pursue a career in broadcast journalism. I got solid foundational training at Marshall University and, on graduation, landed my first TV job as a news producer for WOUB-TV, the PBS station at Ohio University. Because it was a part-time job, I had time to take more classes and, after a couple of years, earned a master's degree in journalism.

When I began looking for a full-time television job in 1986, I was willing to go anywhere. Fortunately, I didn't have to go far. I was hired to be the eastern Kentucky bureau chief for WCHS-TV in Charleston, West Virginia. It sounds more glamorous than it was. Basically, I was assigned a camera and a car and instructed to rent an apartment in Paintsville, Kentucky, nearly two hours away from the station. It was too much responsibility for a kid just out of college, to be sent off alone without much guidance or interaction with more seasoned journalists. If I submitted a story from eastern Kentucky each day, I was fulfilling my duties. Some days, it was easy. Stories about flooding, forest fires, groundbreakings, and drug busts almost wrote themselves. But there were days when I didn't have any idea what to report about. I would drive down back roads, hoping I would see something interesting that could be turned into a story.

The scavenger hunts often paid off. I did stories about what it was like to live in homes accessible only by swinging bridges and discovered a still-active one-room schoolhouse. I was able to get poetic by doing an essay on autumn after gathering lots of video of colorful trees on a particularly beautiful day. One day, I came on a Roman Catholic priest with a megaphone, preaching the gospel along the roadside in a former coal camp to anyone who would listen. These were the stories I loved to tell. Someone else could follow court cases, political scandals, and petition drives.

So I always hoped in the back of my mind that someday I would get a chance to do my own "on the road" type of segment.

That chance came in 1993, when I was working as a reporter for WLEX-TV, the NBC affiliate in Lexington, Kentucky. Each of the reporters was asked to pitch ideas for stories that could be done during sweeps, that time of year when Nielsen measured television viewership. That is when you would see a lot of promotion for stories meant to increase audience size—stories such as "What Are the Germiest Things in Your House?" or "Burglars Reveal How They Picked Their Victims" or "Radon: The Silent Killer."

I pitched my "off the beaten path" idea, asking my managers to give me a week when I would present five feature stories about interesting people or places in Kentucky. The reasoning was simple: "People accuse us of only telling bad news. Let's prove them wrong."

To my surprise, they agreed. In fact, they said that instead of doing five stories in one week, I should make it a series that would run every Friday. I was elated. We just had to have a name for the series. I had trouble coming up with one I really liked that hadn't been used elsewhere, so our assistant news director suggested *Spirit of the Bluegrass*. I didn't really like that, either. I thought it sounded like the name of a train or an airplane. But that is what the promotions team ran with, and I wasn't about to argue.

I did those segments every Friday for two years, covering such things as the Hillbilly Days Festival in Pikeville, ghost stories at Halloween, and what it was like to be a window washer on the outside of skyscrapers. It was the most rewarding work I had ever done, and I worked with an excellent videographer who was just as into it as I was.

But in 1995, I changed jobs, becoming an anchor for a newly launched newscast on WDKY-TV, the FOX affiliate in Lexington, better known as FOX 56. I still went out in the field, but it was "general assignment" reporting. My franchise series had ended.

In 2016, the general manager of FOX 56 came to me, asking if I had any ideas for some type of reports I could do on a regular basis that would help us stand out from the other stations in the city. Of course, I did. I told her about *Spirit of the Bluegrass* and decided it would be fine to use that name again. It had not been copyrighted, and WLEX had not used it in the twenty years since I had left there.

But there was one difference. I wanted to do it all myself. Staffing was tight, and videographers were often hustled from one story to the next with little time in between. I wanted this reincarnation of *Spirit of the Bluegrass* to be the best I could make it. If I knew of a good story that happened only on a Saturday, a Sunday, or a holiday, I wanted to be able to do it. If it required multiple days or going to several locations to tell it right, I wanted that freedom. I was willing to go early in the morning or late at night. I didn't want to have to be at the mercy of another person's schedule.

I asked my general manager to set me up with my own camera gear (tripod, lights, microphones) and committed to returning to my Paintsville days as a "one-man-band" reporter. *Spirit of the Bluegrass* would be my baby. I would set up all the stories, shoot them, write the scripts, and do all the editing. I wanted to be able to go anywhere in the state. To me, the term "Bluegrass" meant all of Kentucky, not just the region around Lexington.

And that is how it happened. I know I am blessed to have so much freedom in my job and to have the trust of my bosses that I will find stories worth telling. I have no one to blame but myself if the video is shaky, the sound breaks up, or the lighting could be better. Every road trip is a learning experience. There are much better videographers than me, but I am a lot better than I used to be. There are better editors, but I love that part of the job. I do believe I have become very good at one thing—recognizing a good story when I see one.

People often ask, "How do you come up with story ideas?" That is not a problem. I keep a folder full of notes, newspaper clippings, internet articles, and letters from viewers. At any time, there are a hundred or so possible stories in the folder. The problem is finding the time to do them. But I try, one week at a time, to share a little bit of the sights, sounds, emotions, and feel of that intangible thing I have come to know and appreciate as *Spirit of the Bluegrass*.

ॐ

The stories that follow are presented as they aired on television, with information that was current at the time. Updated details have been added where appropriate.

SPIRITED PLACES

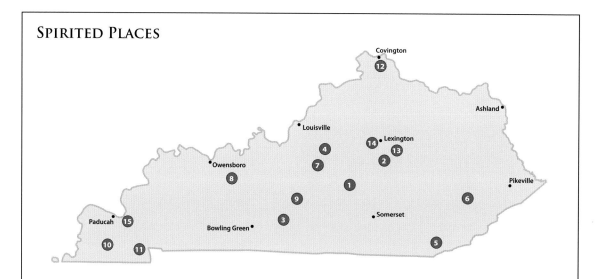

1. Penn's Store, *Gravel Switch*
2. Newby Country Store, *Madison County*
3. Wigwam Village No. 2, *Cave City*
4. Deere John Ranch, *Nelson County*
5. Chained Rock, *Pineville*
6. Mother Goose Inn, *Hazard*
7. Abbey of Gethsemani, *Nelson County*
8. Birthplace of Bluegrass, *Rosine*
9. Kentucky's Stonehenge, *Munfordville*
10. Wooldridge Monuments, *Mayfield*
11. The Shoe Tree, *Murray*
12. Vent Haven, *Fort Mitchell*
13. Clays Ferry Overlook, *Madison County*
14. Fairway to Heaven, *Lexington*
15. Apple Valley Hillbilly Garden and Toyland, *Calvert City*

SPIRITED PLACES

PENN'S STORE

GRAVEL SWITCH

The website for Penn's Store says it is not the easiest place to find. That is an understatement. To the unknowing passerby, the rustic building that sits way back in a field along Highway 243, three miles southeast of Gravel Switch, may look abandoned. Its porch is sagging, the roof is rusty, the signs on the sides are faded. A sane builder would go crazy if he or she put a level to the walls or floors. Most days, there are no signs of life around the old shack.

But on Saturday and Sunday afternoons and some other special days, there is smoke coming from the chimney and music playing on the porch. The field on the other side of the gravel access road is filled with cars.

Musicians play on the porch at Penn's Store as community members and tourists linger to listen.

Penn's Store becomes a gathering place for this community that straddles three county lines—Boyle, Casey, and Marion. A building in the middle of nowhere becomes the center of a lot of action.

Records show the store has been around since at least 1845, when it was owned by a twenty-one-year-old man named William Spragens. Gabriel Jackson Penn bought it in 1850, and there has been a Penn in charge ever since, making it the oldest store in the country continuously owned by the same family.

Dawn Osborn is the current owner-operator. Gabriel Jackson Penn was her great-great-great grandfather.

The country store has a little bit of everything and not a lot of anything. If you want cigarettes or shoe polish, soap, or pickled eggs, you can find those things here. The store still even has penny candy. But it is not a place where customers grab and go. They usually sit and chat around the wood-burning stove or take part in the music sessions on the porch. Anyone who comes with an instrument is welcome to join in or offer up a solo.

Don't expect the store to get a facelift anytime soon. Osborn knows she would be in trouble with the locals if she tried to modernize it. A few years ago, she fixed a hole in the front screen door and took some criticism for it. The often-repeated joke was that the hole was there so the flies could get out.

"The store really almost has a soul of its own," Osborn said. "I want people to experience what someone one hundred years ago experienced when they walk through that door."

A century ago, there were more buildings around Penn's Store, including a chicken coop because people would trade chickens for goods. But perhaps the most important structure came in 1992, when they built an outhouse, the store's first-ever public restroom. Penn's Privy was the subject of magazine articles around the world and led to a festival called the "Great Outhouse Blowout." It attracted four thousand visitors.

That exposure brought more tourists, so today, many of the products on the shelves are geared toward one-time visitors—souvenir items such as T-shirts, caps, and mugs. Osborn said she has welcomed visitors from all fifty states and more than twenty countries. The store is equal parts neighborhood market, gift shop, museum, and gathering place.

Tony Cooper, a musician who often plays guitar on the porch, said he always feels as if he is home when he is at the store. "It's just a wonderful place to come," Cooper said. "They'll treat you so many ways, you got to like one of them. I'd love to see it stay here another two hundred years."

It may not last that long, but Osborn's daughter, Olivia Graas, often works behind the counter and plans to be the seventh-generation Penn to keep the tradition alive in some form or fashion even though she is also going to law school.

"I do have my own aspirations," Graas said. "But at the end of the day, I think Penn's Store is something that's going to be kept in this family for a long, long time."

That's music to the ears of longtime patrons who can't imagine a future without this reminder of the past.

NEWBY COUNTRY STORE

MADISON COUNTY

A country store is the heart of Newby, a small community about nine miles west of Richmond. Local folks walk there to get lunch or just to talk to their neighbors on the porch. One three-year-old boy often arrives on his toy tractor, while his dad follows behind on an all-terrain vehicle. But in recent years, Newby Country Store has also become a destination for tourists. On many days, cars line both sides of Newby Road just outside the store.

Ashlie Hatton, who co-owns the store with her husband, Brad, said, "I think the biggest comment we get all the time is it just feels like a step back in time."

The store has been in operation since 1891 but was in danger of closing in 2020 before the Hattons stepped in to buy it.

"We bought it to save it," said Ashlie. "Then we just met some of the greatest people, and one thing led to another. Here we are, years later, and it's like our heart and soul."

Because the store has operated continuously for more than 130 years, the owners get away with some things a new business could not, such as having gas pumps right by the side of the narrow country road. If a driver is pulled up to the pumps, other cars must veer to the road's center to avoid them.

That was one feature that was grandfathered in by code enforcement officers. Also, the store does not have indoor plumbing. Water is carried in from a well and boiled so that the owners can keep the store's lunch counter open. The stacked ham and cheese sandwiches are a popular item.

Ashlie said, "If we start to do anything to the building, then we have to bring it up to current codes. We would lose our gas pumps, for sure. We would have to code everything, and it would basically lose its nostalgia, I believe."

Newby Country Store has been in continuous operation since 1891.
ASHLIE HATTON

Longtime resident Don Long has visited the store almost daily for more than seventy years. His parents owned it for a few years back in the 1980s. He has lots of memories about how it used to be.

"Yeah, I remember when a Coca-Cola was a nickel, candy was a nickel, and gas was thirty cents a gallon," he said. He used to know everyone who came in the door and marvels at the number of strangers who stop these days, those who see the store as an attraction. Many tourists arrive after crossing the Kentucky River on the Valley View Ferry, which has been in operation since 1785, seven years before Kentucky was admitted to the Union.

"I never imagined it would ever be like this," Long said.

The store used to carry most of the provisions a farmer would want. Now it is more of a gift shop, featuring Kentucky-made products such as candles and soap, beer cheese and honey, clothing, and vintage candy. It carries more than sixty specialty sodas in glass bottles.

On many summer nights, there are concerts on the porch. Visitors watch and listen from a field on the other side of the road, not bothered that an occasional car passes in front of the performers.

Ashlie is a Richmond native who moved back to the area after living for twenty years in Florida, where she worked in medical sales. She never planned on being a shopkeeper after she retired.

"We never dreamed it would be one of the most amazing things we've ever done," she said.

People around Newby are certainly glad the new owners know how to market the market. They can't imagine their community without it.

WIGWAM VILLAGE NO. 2

CAVE CITY

Wigwam Village No. 2 is a blast from the past.

"I'll never forget the first time I pulled up and saw it," said co-owner Megan Smith. "It was awesome!"

More than eight decades after it was built, the roadside motel is still a traffic stopper.

Fifteen concrete teepees make up Wigwam Village No. 2, a unique motel that has welcomed guests since 1937. DON E. YEOMAN JR.

A guest with an artsy car parked outside Wigwam Village No. 2 in the summer of 2023. KEITH STONE

Keith Stone surprised Smith with a romantic getaway trip to Wigwam Village in 2020.

"When we arrived, it was my first time here," she said. "My mind was blown, and Keith said, 'Well, you know it's for sale!'" That set the wheels in motion for the Louisville couple to become the new owners of an iconic motor lodge that was built in 1937. They said that when they found out their bid to buy it was accepted, it was like winning the lottery.

Renovating the property has been a labor of love. Stone said he has not yet come across the blueprints as he goes through records associated with the motel, but he believes they will turn up one day. Because he and Smith have backgrounds in architecture, they have a good idea of how the fifteen concrete teepees should be repaired. They do have the original patent, which has been a help as they rework some features inside the rooms, adding modern safety and energy-saving features while keeping the original look and feel.

Inside the rounded walls of each teepee, you will find either one or two beds, a small dresser, and a bathroom with a shower. The furniture and bathroom tiles are original from 1937, but the mattresses are new, as are the flat-screen TVs. Although travelers can't wait to see inside the rooms, the new owners believe a lot of the experience of staying there has always happened outside the cone-shaped structures.

Stone said, "People would spend a lot of time in the area we call 'the bowl.' They would play games and picnic and make bonfires. Then the weirdest thing would happen—people would start talking to each other!"

The owners say it still happens today. They make a nightly bonfire in the conversation pit to encourage guests to come out of their teepees and get to know each other.

By 1949, there were seven Wigwam Villages around the nation. The first one was just up the road in Horse Cave. Just three remain—No. 2 in Cave City; No. 6 in Holbrook, Arizona; and No. 7 in San Bernardino, California. The two in the west are along the historic Route 66. This one attracted families headed to nearby Mammoth Cave.

They were the brainchild of businessman Frank Redford, who wanted his motels to stand out from all the others popping up in the middle of the twentieth century, when auto touring was just becoming popular. Stone said Redford initially got some things wrong.

"These do not look like wigwams. They look like teepees. He did not like the sound of Teepee Village, so he renamed it," Stone said. Traditional wigwams are dome shaped. Neither wigwams nor teepees were used by indigenous people in Kentucky.

Stone and Smith are sensitive to the fact that building such a motel today would be seen as offensive. They try hard to balance preservation with political correctness. In past decades, the motel's gift shop sold such things as plastic tomahawks and toy feather headdresses. There is nothing like that for sale now. The owners do not market a stay at the village as a Native American experience even though Redford did. They celebrate it as an architectural wonder and piece of Americana from the early days of road travel.

"We think those things help to counterbalance the cultural appropriation and swing the pendulum back to Wigwam Village No. 2 being worth preserving and restoring," Stone said.

Plus, Smith adds, "They're just so darn cute!"

The property is listed on the National Register of Historic Places. The new owners have plans to turn the large teepee (they call it the "Big Wam") that used to house the office and a restaurant into a coffee shop.

Wigwam Village No. 2 has been described in a lot of ways over the decades: tacky and wacky, fascinating and fun. It is good to know this piece of the past has a future thanks to new owners who love everything about it.

"We watch the public drive by, and you see those mouths open, and you can read their lips saying, 'This is amazing.' It happens every day," Smith said.

"So, if you're wondering why someone would want to buy this place and restore it, my main answer would be, 'Who wouldn't want to?'"

DEERE JOHN RANCH

NELSON COUNTY

Bloomfield sits just off the Bluegrass Parkway, a town with about a thousand residents. Unlike many small towns, it still has a vibrant business district. There is Nettie Jarvis Antiques, a well-known shop that is like a museum, connected to a general store and tearoom, and Olde Bloomfield Meeting Hall, which houses an ice cream shop, bowling alley, and tavern.

All of these old structures have new life thanks to one woman, Linda Bruckheimer, the wife of famed Hollywood producer Jerry Bruckheimer. While he made blockbuster movies over the years, such as *Black Hawk Down*, *Beverly Hills Cop*, and *Top Gun*, she restored buildings.

A row of partially buried tractors along Kentucky Route 55 near Bloomfield is known as the Deere John Ranch.

"It's hard to close your eyes to something you see and want to do," Linda Bruckheimer said. "Eventually, there will be more things."

The Bruckheimers own a large farm just outside Bloomfield, a town founded in 1790. Linda also pursues her passion for preservation there. She has restored several cabins on the property as places for their celebrity friends to stay when they visit from Hollywood. One of the cabins predates Abraham Lincoln.

Linda, who grew up in Louisville, discovered Bloomfield on a drive years before she ever dreamed of living there. As an author and photographer, she likes to take the back roads to seek out unusual things. Her love of roadside attractions led her to create her own in the summer of 2020, just a couple of miles from her downtown strip of businesses.

Drivers who enter Bloomfield from the west on State Route 55 pass the couple's farm, and many do a double-take when they see the green scene beyond the white-planked fences.

"It's one more thing to make Bloomfield unique," Bruckheimer said.

The field looks like a graveyard for John Deere tractors, ten of them in a row, partially buried with their noses pointed skyward. Bruckheimer said she was inspired by a quirky attraction she loves in Texas known as Cadillac Ranch. It prompted her to design her so-called Deere John Ranch, a tribute to the region's farming history.

"A lot of people are going in a car. They don't want to be just on the freeway. They want to see the things that make Kentucky 'Kentucky,' and you never know what that is," she said. "It's just something unexpected."

The tractors were planted without fanfare. They just showed up for people to discover on their own and are lined up from the oldest to the newest. Bruckheimer says it is art, so the key is to get people to notice it even if they don't understand it.

"I think it gives people a lift and puts a smile on their face, and that's the most important thing to me."

Even when she is away at her primary home in Los Angeles, Linda Bruckheimer is always looking for ways to promote Bloomfield, and she believes retired tractors can still have a lot of pull.

CHAINED ROCK

PINEVILLE

You might call Pineville a sleepy town at the base of a mountain. But a century ago, people had trouble sleeping there. A big rock was to blame for the insomnia.

"The legend went that at any time, this big boulder could fall off the mountain to crush the town, and for a lot of the town's children, that was terrifying," said Keith Bowling, the naturalist at Pine Mountain State Park.

So the big rock prompted some little white lies. Children were told not to worry because it was chained up there. That story spread, and visitors started to ask the locals why they couldn't see the chain. Thus, the tall tale turned into a public relations stunt.

In 1933, a committee enlisted members of the Kiwanis Club, the Boy Scouts, and the Civilian Conservation Corps to construct an unnatural wonder. The group obtained a giant chain from an abandoned steam shovel at a coal mine site in Virginia and, with a team of mules, dragged it up the mountain. Reportedly, the chain had to be cut in half to be pulled up the mountain in two trips. It was welded together again at the top. Bowling has heard it took fifty men to heave the chain from a cliff to the rock and anchor it with giant bolts. The chain is 101 feet long and weighs a ton.

The story of how the Chained Rock Club saved the town from "imminent disaster" was reported in hundreds of daily newspapers across the country. But, in truth, Pineville was never in danger of being crushed by the rock.

Bowling said it is a geological optical illusion. "It's actually where big flat sheets of rock have curled up on each end and we're seeing a piece of sandstone just jutting out. It's all actually interconnected, so what looks like a boulder at the top is just a sheet of exposed rock."

Visitors to Pine Mountain State Park can hike to see Chained Rock.
ANDREW NEIKIRK

Visitors to the park today can take a half-mile trail to the rock to see the chain, the city below, and a splendid view of the surrounding Cumberland Mountains. You can get as close to the edge as you dare. Bowling said people make the hike the first time because of the legend but often come back multiple times because of the vista.

People who take the hike are amazed by how massive the chain is but wonder if it was worth the effort to lug it up the mountain.

Sarah Lamm, a Georgia resident who visited in 2017, stood on the rock and said, "I guess it's better safe than sorry. It doesn't look like it's going to fall, but I guess if you lived down there, you might feel a little more secure if you knew it was chained."

You don't have to take the trail to see the chain. It is clearly visible by looking up from almost any street in Pineville. For many people, fiction became fact, and tourists do come because of these links to the past.

MOTHER GOOSE INN

HAZARD

The Mother Goose Inn may be Kentucky's most unusual house.

As the story goes, sometime in the 1930s, Hazard businessman George Stacy was having a Thanksgiving dinner that included a cooked goose. He reportedly was fascinated by the shape of the carcass and told his wife, Ollie, "I'm going to build a house that looks like this."

Visitors to Hazard have been fascinated by the Mother Goose Inn since 1940. The once-private home can now be booked for overnight stays. BAILEY RICHARDS

Whatever the inspiration, he did indeed build a goose-shaped house, which was completed in 1940. The house was always a private residence, but Stacy knew it would attract people to his businesses. Over the years, he ran a market, a diner, and a gas station just down the hill from the house from a companion building shaped like a basket of eggs.

Some of the features of the goose-like house are egg-shaped windows, feathered shingles, and green eyes that used to light up (made from the reflectors in a traffic light). Late in 2020, the family teamed up with Sherry Spradlin to bring the house back to its 1940s condition, with all the furnishings inside from that period. Spradlin, who owns the nearby Harmony House Bed and Breakfast, also arranges rentals at the Mother Goose Inn. It has three bedrooms, one bathroom, a living room, and a kitchen. Guests can also go up into the attic and see the timbers that make up the ribs of the goose. There are some historic pictures on display in the attic as well.

Spradlin offers tours of the inn on certain days of the week for a small admission fee to help pay for upkeep. If you're lucky, your tour guide could be Alice McIntosh, a Stacy family member who used to live in the house, or her niece, Raegan Francis, who dresses in clothes from the 1940s as she recounts the history of the house.

Francis says she remembers having many sleepovers at the house as a child, saying her friends "thought it was the best thing in the world."

On March 24, 2021, the head of the Mother Goose Inn fell off due to damage it suffered over the years from rain and snow. McIntosh vowed that "the goose will rise again," and many people in Perry County donated money to help with its renovation. The rebuilt head was put back in place on August 27, 2021.

Because this house is centered on the theme of "Mother Goose," I thought it would be fun to try to tell the story in rhyme. I challenged myself to even make the sound bites from interviews fit into the poetic narrative. Here is the script I came up with for our newscast:

In the city of Hazard, Kentucky, there's an inn that's really
*   quite ducky.*
The kitchen is neat, the bedrooms are sweet;
If you stay there, you'll likely feel lucky.
But on the outside, it's rather absurd.
My word, it looks like a bird!
The builder must've had a screw loose
To design a house while eating a goose.
An idea for the birdies, it started in the thirties.
George Stacy's Thanksgiving dinner was great,
Inspiration came on like a light.
He liked what he saw on his plate.

Raegan: *"Mind you, he was drinking a little bit that night."*

The plans came together rather quickly—
A rocky nest, an egg-shaped pane.
His wife, Ollie, watched it all unfold.

Raegan: *"She thought he was absolutely insane!"*

But seven years later, the goose house was cooked.
It had fine-feathered features everywhere anyone looked.
It has traffic lights for eyes
That used to glow with bright green glares.

Sherry: *"We hope to have that feature back soon—*
As soon as we can do some more repairs."

Sherry Spradlin now manages The Goose
As a bed and breakfast nest.
Alice McIntosh and her niece, Raegan, give tours.
They know the place the best.
Their family tree includes the Stacys,
The home's history they can produce.

Raegan: *"If you look into the corner of this room*
You see stairs that lead to the head of The Goose."
The attic shows the structure's spine

Raegan:	*"Is actually an inverted boat."*
	There's a museum up there, with pictures that share
	How they've kept The Goose afloat.

Although it was always foremost a home,
There was roadside business each day of the week;
A market, a gas station, a place to buy lunch,

| Sherry: | *"It is very, very unique."* |
| | *—with a beak!* |

Many visitors to Hazard are surprised to find this when they meander.
Others have heard all about it and come just to give it a gander.

The private home often brought the uninvited

| Alice: | *"There are a lot of people just wanting to see the inside."* |

So, there's a fowl crowd that's really egg-cited
Now that the doors have opened wide.

Visitors are flocking from all over the world.
They get goosebumps from all that they're shown.
They'll long remember this flight of fancy.

| Raegan: | *"They just see this, and their minds are blown!"* |

The house has won newfound devotion
Just like it had back in the day.
It was not a bird-brained notion.

| Sherry: | *"We'd love for you to come and stay!"* |

If you can't stop for a visit, at least give a honk as you pass.
I'm Marvin Bartlett in Hazard, with the Spirit of the Bluegrass.

ABBEY OF GETHSEMANI

NELSON COUNTY

Every day, seven times a day, forty-some Trappist monks go to a chapel to pray at the Abbey of Gethsemani. It is a practice that has been unbroken since 1848.

"It's just part of the total energy of the church that there are people giving themselves body, soul, and heart to a life of prayer," said Brother Paul Quenon, a monk who has been at the abbey for more than fifty years.

It is a peaceful, structured life, with the first prayers coming at 3 a.m. Brother Paul said the early start to the day is essential to contemplative life. "It's quiet. You don't have pressure to get work done."

Trappist monks take fruitcakes out of the oven at the Gethsemani Farms bakery, dozens at a time.

Yes, he mentioned work. The monks must support themselves, and they have found a sweet way to pay the bills by making fudge and fruitcakes so good that it is almost sinful.

"These products are our living," said Brother Roger Kaler, manager of Gethsemani Farms. "We sell them to pay our hospital bills, doctor bills, electric bills, all the needs the monks require."

Every monk who is able spends time in the bakery or shipping room. They turn out rich fudge in many flavors. Many of the recipes include a favorite local ingredient, Kentucky bourbon. In the fall, fruitcake production ramps up. The cakes come out of the large oven dozens at a time, as gift orders begin to come in for the holidays.

Brother Roger said they make about seventy thousand pounds of fudge each year and about the same amount of fruitcake. Their work is not just for income. The monks at the Abbey of Gethsemani see manual labor as a requirement for their lifestyle.

"If we're sitting around all day praying, the prayers would tend to dry up," said Brother Paul. "So, the value of work is not only to give you variation in activity, but it's very important to engage the body and rest the mind."

This old place has modern touches. In fact, the fudge and fruitcake business would not thrive if not for a first-class shipping operation, and internet sales have been a godsend.

In recent years, the abbey has added a gift shop. Even though much of the monastery is off-limits, the monks welcome nearly nine thousand visitors a year, many who come on retreat for a taste of the peaceful life. Visitors are also welcome to drop in on any of the seven daily prayer services, often watching from the chapel balcony. It is mesmerizing to listen to their melodic chants.

Many people are drawn to the abbey because of its association with one of the most famous monks of modern times, social activist and author Thomas Merton, who lived here from 1941 until his death in 1968. His grave is marked with a cross that looks like all the others in the cemetery, inscribed with his monastic name, Fr. Louis Merton.

Visitors are free to roam many wooded trails outside the gates of the monastery. The working farm takes up two thousand acres. If you come on a monk while exploring, know that many of them still prefer silence as much as possible. It is best to go to the visitor center to ask questions and learn more about monastic life.

The brothers have learned the value of marketing, even for fruitcake, something people either love or hate.

"Even if you don't like it, you might know someone who does," Brother Roger said with a wink. He devises marketing campaigns all year round, making sure the treats are considered as gifts outside the Christmas season. Valentine's Day and Mother's Day are also big occasions for advertising the fudge.

The sweet products are a link to the outside world—maybe a way to let people know that the men who make these treats are praying for them, every day inside the gates of Gethsemani.

"We live close to God," said Brother Paul. "That's why we came here, and, hopefully, that's what we're finding."

BIRTHPLACE OF BLUEGRASS

ROSINE

A small wooden house on a ridge in Ohio County may not seem all that special at first glance, but if the walls could talk, well, they wouldn't. They would sing.

The boyhood home of bluegrass music legend Bill Monroe is a must-see attraction for devotees of the genre. They call it "ground zero"—the place where country music was twisted and shaped into a different sound that came to be known as bluegrass.

The home, which was built in 1917, stood abandoned for decades and was on the verge of collapse when some people in Rosine got serious about saving it in the 1990s. The first time I visited the house was just as

Members of King's Highway play on the porch of the Bill Monroe Homeplace.

the talk of restoration was beginning. I paid a farmer $20 to take me to the house. He hitched a wagon to his tractor and hauled me and a videographer through woods and an overgrown field to the top of Jerusalem Ridge. There was not a clear path to the crumbling house and no signs indicating it was a historic property.

When work finally began—and not a minute too soon—Bill Monroe himself met with the restoration crews to make sure the paint colors were correct and to tell them how furniture was arranged in the house he once shared with his parents, five brothers, and two sisters. He died in 1996 before the house was opened to the public. It was finally ready in 2001, and since then, tourists have come by the busloads.

Monroe was born in 1911 in another house nearby but moved with his family into the house on Jerusalem Ridge when he was five. It is known as The Homeplace. Historians say it was the place Monroe had in mind when he wrote his classic song "I'm On My Way Back to the Old Home." The home was part of an eight-hundred-acre farm where the family raised tobacco, corn, cattle, and chickens.

It is also where Monroe learned to love music. His mother's brother, James Pendleton Vandiver, often visited there and played his fiddle for the children. Monroe memorialized him in the song "Uncle Pen."

Jody Flener, executive director of Ohio County's Tourism Commission, loves to watch when visitors come to The Homeplace. For many of them, it is a pilgrimage.

"Everybody's like, 'This is land Bill walked on. Bill played in these woods. Bill was here,'" she said. "I have actually seen people get out and kiss the ground. It's sort of the Memphis of bluegrass."

It is not unusual to drive up to the house and see musicians playing on the porch.

"Everybody loves coming here," said Josh Johnson, a member of the bluegrass band King's Highway. "It's just a very special place to play music. It sounds better here!"

It's difficult to define bluegrass music, but some of its characteristics are high-pitched vocals, offbeat rhythm, and the freedom performers have to improvise.

But if you can't play bluegrass music, you can hear it just about anywhere in Rosine. It doesn't get any more traditional than the free Friday night shows at Rosine Barn, a rustic structure that sits along the main road through the town of four hundred people. The barn was named by the *New York Times* as "one of the places to see in 2016." Not a week goes by that the house band doesn't play Monroe's most famous song, "Blue Moon of Kentucky."

Flener says it is common on a summer evening when the barn doors are open to see the parking lot filled with strangers in lawn chairs.

"You lean over and ask, 'Where are you from?,' and they may say France, Sweden, or Germany," Flener said. "It's terribly exciting for us to have these people come to our town."

Although small, Rosine has learned to market itself and now offers a complete bluegrass music experience. The Bill Monroe Museum was built in 2018 and is full of artifacts from the career of the man who became known as the "Father of Bluegrass Music." Fans can see clothing Monroe wore on stage as well as awards he won over the years, instruments, albums, and antique furniture from his home. They can also visit Uncle Pen's cabin, where young Bill learned to play many instruments as a teenager.

Monroe is buried in Rosine Cemetery along with his parents, siblings, and Uncle Pen. It is another place pickers come to play out of respect. A visitor shouldn't be surprised to see someone strumming a banjo or mandolin at the foot of Monroe's monument.

Bluegrass music has seen a resurgence in recent years, but in Rosine, it has always been alive and pickin'.

Said Flener, "This place should be full of music all the time."

KENTUCKY'S STONEHENGE

MUNFORDVILLE

England's Stonehenge has stood for thousands of years, a mysterious and massive monument. There is debate about who built it and why. But there is no doubt who built Kentucky's smaller-scaled version.

It is the work of Chester Fryer, the former mayor of Munfordville. He was eighty-seven years old when I visited him in 2021 and still a bundle of energy.

Chester Fryer said he searched a thousand acres to find rocks to build his version of Stonehenge. WAYNE GARMON

In 2000, Fryer started bringing large stones to the ten-acre lot around his home. He had never been to the real Stonehenge, but the pictures he called up on his computer screen rocked his world. After seeing the images, he said he felt compelled by unknown forces to re-create the ancient landmark.

"That sounds crazy, I know," Fryer said. "Is it the magnetic pull or God or somebody else who wanted me to build it? I know it's something special."

So special that it has become a tourist attraction.

He said about thirty to forty people stop by every day, and he welcomes them as long as they don't climb on the structures or leave trash. Kentucky's Stonehenge is easy to find just off Interstate 65. There is no charge to walk around the property, although visitors can put donations in a small box beside the driveway.

Hazel Ramos and her family from Indiana discovered the creation after reading about it during a Google search for day trips. They spent more than an hour taking selfies among the stones. "We like to find things like this," she said. "It makes some good memories for the family."

This Stonehenge does not strictly follow the specifications of the original, but Fryer said he used a compass to place the stones in a way that ensures that shadows fall through the center of the configuration during the summer and winter solstices.

Stonehenge is just part of Fryer's rock garden. There is a large cross carved of stone, rocks that look like cannons positioned on a mock battlefield, and boulders Fryer collected just because he liked the way they look.

"I've always liked rocks," he said. "I walked over a thousand acres collecting these rocks."

He did almost all the work himself, moving the rocks with a tractor and lifting them with a front loader. He said he didn't want someone else to tell him how it should be done. He laments the fact that he doesn't have the strength he did when he started this project. If he did, he said he would keep adding to his field of dreams. "If I was young, I could really build something," he said.

Some say the original Stonehenge is magical, but so is the one in Munfordville. It stacks up well when it comes to curiosities and accomplishments.

Chester Fryer died on July 1, 2022 at age eighty-eight and was buried in the Munford-ville Municipal Cemetery beneath a rock tombstone he carved for himself. Visitors are still welcome to see his version of Stonehenge at 201 Lynn Avenue.

WOOLDRIDGE MONUMENTS

MAYFIELD

In many ways, Maplewood Cemetery looks like any other memorial park, with its rows of tombstones topped with angels, crosses, and urns. But among the silent stones, one plot almost screams for attention. It is known as the "Strange Procession That Never Moves."

According to tourism director Cynthia Elder, the most popular tourist attraction in Graves County is a grave.

Eighteen statues crowd the burial plot of Henry Wooldridge, making up a scene referred to as the "Strange Procession That Never Moves."

MAYFIELD-GRAVES COUNTY TOURISM COMMISSION

"We've had people come from as far as Europe and Asia to see the monuments," she said.

The crowded collection of statues marks the grave of Henry Wooldridge, a Mayfield man who died in 1899. His likeness stands at a lectern, carved in Italian marble. He is also carved in limestone astride his favorite horse. That statue is surrounded by figures of his mother, four brothers, three sisters, two great nieces, two hunting dogs, a deer, and a fox.

"I think, being eccentric, he just hoarded his money through the years and really didn't have anything to spend it on," Elder said. "He decided to do this, and nobody questioned him. He just did it himself."

Wooldridge, who made his fortune as a horse trader, began installing statues five years before his death, and over time, the plot thickened. It is a grave site full of mystery. Why did the lifelong bachelor not include a likeness of his father? Why did he immortalize only two of his many nieces and nephews? Why are all eighteen statues looking off into the distance rather than at each other? We may never know.

Descendants have written that Wooldridge had plans for more statues. If he had lived past the age of seventy-seven, there is no telling how long this stationary parade would have stretched. Eighteen statues were completed, with most of them being created by a stonecutter in Paducah. The grave site is listed on the National Register of Historic Places.

"I think he was a proud man—proud of himself—and that is why he had the things he loved the most featured in his burial plot," Elder said.

In 2009, an ice storm brought an oak tree crashing down on the monuments, causing considerable damage. The heads and limbs were broken off many statues. The city and federal emergency funds provided $100,000 to repair the limestone lineup. The plot was unscathed by a tornado that destroyed much of Mayfield in December 2021.

"We might laugh about it, and we might make fun of it, but it's still our monument. We would hate to see it go," Elder said.

They say dead men tell no tales, but visitors would really like to know what Henry Wooldridge was trying to say when he turned his final resting place into a place where no one seems at rest.

THE SHOE TREE

MURRAY

The Quad at Murray State University (MSU) is the heart of the campus, seemingly watched over by a statue of the school's founder, Rainey T. Wells. It is a statue that appears to stare straight at a strange tree, rooted in love and covered with shoes.

"When two students meet and fall in love on campus and end up marrying, it's good luck and tradition to come back and put your shoes on the tree," said Darren Jones.

So that is exactly what Darren and his wife, Danette, did.

"It was twenty-five years after the fact, but we finally got them up there," Darren said.

The former campus sweethearts brought their two daughters to the tree on Valentine's Day in 2017 so that they could watch as their parents added their shoes to the lovely landmark.

"It was very special," Danette said, "something my children will remember, and we can remember always."

The tradition began in the 1960s, but no one is sure how. It may have been an art project, an act of vandalism, or a way for a boy to tiptoe his way into a girl's heart.

If their tongues could talk, every shoe on the tree would have a story. That is something MSU's alumni relations director said she thought about on the first day she started working on campus in 2016.

"I just felt so lucky and blessed to be part of this tradition and the heritage," Carrie McGinnis said. "I would take one look at the tree and get teary-eyed. I'm not embarrassed to say it."

The Shoe Tree has been called one of the quirkiest college traditions in the United States. MURRAY STATE UNIVERSITY

The tree that stands in the Quad now is the third one to host the shoes. The first one caught fire after being struck by lightning. And the second one was taken down in 2015, when the weight on the limbs became a safety hazard.

"If you can imagine, our maintenance team at MSU carefully took each of the shoes that was salvageable and moved them from that tree to this tree as best they could to keep preserving that tradition," McGinnis said.

The current tree is all trunk. The branches have been cut off so that all shoes can be attached only to the strongest part of the mighty oak. Couples who put their tennis shoes, flip-flops, boots, or loafers on the tree are affectionately known as "solemates."

In 2023, *U.S. News and World Report* listed MSU's Shoe Tree as one of the quirkiest college traditions in the country.

Who says love doesn't grow on trees? The stories and photos behind the campus tradition are shared on the tree's own Facebook page (*Murray State University Shoe Tree*). Often, baby shoes get added to the mix. For countless couples, the best walk down memory lane goes past a tree with no limbs but a lot of heart.

Danette said, "Each time we come back to campus, we always check to make sure the shoes are still there."

VENT HAVEN

FORT MITCHELL

In a quiet neighborhood in Kenton County, you will find a retirement home. Vent Haven may look small, but there are more than one thousand retirees here—mostly blockheads. It is the world's only museum dedicated to the art of ventriloquism.

The museum houses the collection of William Shakespeare Berger, a businessman who dabbled in ventriloquism and bought his first dummy in 1910. His collection grew rapidly in the 1930s and soon filled his home, his garage, and a shed. He acquired at least five hundred dummies during his lifetime.

Hundreds of wooden dummies sit in silence at Vent Haven in Fort Mitchell.

Throwing your voice was a popular form of entertainment during the vaudeville era, and Berger pulled a lot of strings to collect some of the most famous fake faces of his time. He acquired Charlie McCarthy, the witty sidekick of ventriloquist Edgar Bergen, and Jerry Mahoney, who was brought to life by Paul Winchell in the 1950s. Other notables on display from the golden age of television include Knucklehead Smiff, Lambchop, and Farfel the Dog.

Curator Lisa Sweasy said the museum appeals to visitors of all ages.

"There's a vent [the nickname for a ventriloquist] for every generation," she said. "Often, visitors come down the driveway thinking they don't know any vents. Then they'll see a photo of Shari Lewis or Darci Lynn Farmer or Jeff Dunham or Edgar Bergen and say, 'Oh, I do know them.' Then that's what I focus on in that tour."

The founder died in 1972, but the collection continues to grow. The museum doesn't buy dummies. They have all been donated to live out their days there in the lap of luxury. There are more than 1,150 dummies on display, with the population growing by twenty to thirty each year.

Sweasy knows a lot of people would not want her job. They have seen too many scary movies about dummies coming to life.

"It is a lot of eyeballs looking at you," she admits. "It's one of those things you get used to, and then you're fine. They're not going to move or anything. They're just wood or papier-mâché."

If someone seems nervous about entering a room full of dummies, she shows them the friendliest ones first—funny animals or objects made of foam and fabric. "There's nothing scary about a talking traffic cone or a furry bear," she said.

It is a museum where you look but don't touch. Sweasy realizes it is tempting to pick up a dummy and make it talk, but Berger always said that was disrespectful to the original artists.

"Each of these dummies has a voice and a personality, and a vent worked to develop that," she said. "The operator isn't here, so we do not attempt to be that operator."

Also, these are fragile pieces of entertainment history, with some of them dating back to the Civil War.

The museum closed in 2021 for a $1.2 million renovation. It reopened in 2023 as a fully accessible facility, with better lighting, climate control, educational space, and a sixty-seat theater funded by Jeff Dunham. The building still blends in nicely with the quiet neighborhood. The museum also hosts the annual Vent Haven ConVENTion each summer at a northern Kentucky hotel, which features performances, panel discussions, and workshops.

You have to believe if these characters could speak for themselves, they would love that people still remember when they were full of life.

Sweasy said, "If you're looking to do something that is unique and you can't do anywhere else, Vent Haven is your place to see."

Tours can be booked online at the museum's website (https://www .venthaven.org) from May through September. No walk-ins are permitted.

CLAYS FERRY OVERLOOK

MADISON COUNTY

Jay Webb likes the view from an empty cabin overlooking the Kentucky River. But that view, which includes the impressive Clays Ferry Bridge, was hidden when he bought the property in late 2021.

"Everyone thinks the state owns the property, and they're shocked when I introduce myself as the owner," Webb said.

The Berea man discovered that the four-acre site was for sale while working as a surveyor in the area. It includes a stone-walled overlook built in the 1930s, probably as a project of the Works Progress Administration (WPA).

"I thought someone needed to save it," Webb said. "Sometimes I question, 'Why me?'"

For the past twenty years, people crossing the big Interstate 75 bridge linking Madison and Fayette counties would not have known there was an overlook on the hillside. Drivers couldn't see the stone wall, the cabin, or much of anything else because there was so much overgrowth.

A drive off Exit 97 would have revealed a large illegal dump. "There was no view at all of the river or the bridge," Webb said. "It was completely blocked."

Webb worked with the Madison County judge-executive to get a state grant to clean up the site. He said dump trucks hauled out more than 330 loads of trash over a three-week period. Gradually, the Clays Ferry Bridge, the river, and the original one-lane bridge at the bottom of the gorge came into view.

"We just started trimming trees, cutting bushes, and it keeps going and going," Webb said. Cleaning up the overlook and the hillside above the bridge has become his passion. It is arduous work but a labor of love.

Travelers who stop at the Clays Ferry Overlook can once again see the Interstate 75 bridge that crosses the Kentucky River, a view that was obscured by trees, brush, and trash. JAY WEBB

The cleanup is ongoing but has become much more manageable.

"Once a week or so, I try to pick up a bag of garbage by just walking along the road," Webb said. "The bag's a little lighter each week."

Webb manages a Facebook page for the Clays Ferry Overlook where people share pictures of their visits. Some are recent, others are from decades ago.

He gets emotional when he describes one photograph that was shared. It was the last picture taken of a man who went off to fight in World War II. Webb said he was told the man died storming the beaches of Normandy. The photo will always remind his family of the joyful day their loved one stopped to enjoy the scenery.

"You can look at the old pictures compared to the new, and in both, you see families and children pointing out, looking over the view and looking over the bridge," Webb said. "Everyone seems to smile, so I like that."

Webb has also become a bit of a historian. He knows that there was a ferry crossing the river as early as 1792. Around 1870, a one-lane bridge was built across the river at the bottom of the valley. The first span of the Clays Ferry Bridge was built at the top of the ridges in 1946, and the second came with Interstate 75 in 1963. In the mid-1990s, the two spans were connected to make one solid bridge in what is an architectural marvel. You could not really appreciate the scope of the structure if not for the overlook.

Webb would like to fix up the cabin overlooking the bridge to be something of a mini-museum and visitor's center where travelers could learn some of the history of the area. He is amassing a collection of old postcards and newspaper clippings. But he said it may just be a place where he hangs out during his spare time after he retires, telling stories to anyone who stops and will listen.

There is no real gain for Webb in owning the property except for the joy of knowing he has given people a reason to get off the interstate, even if just for a few minutes. He has created a photo spot or, more accurately, uncovered one.

"It's satisfying when you're done and you can look back and see your accomplishment at the end of the day."

FAIRWAY TO HEAVEN

LEXINGTON

The Lexington Ice Center is known as "a cool place for fun." But in the summer, there is more action outside the main entrance on a miniature golf course known as Fairway to Heaven. It is somewhat out of sight, tucked away in a Lexington neighborhood away from the main thoroughfares, but plenty of people seek it out for a unique way to combine golf and gospel.

Emma Penrose of Dayton, Ohio, was one of those pilgrims. She joined a friend to play all fifty-four holes on the course, which is divided into three sections: Old Testament, New Testament, and Miracles.

The most difficult hole at Fairway to Heaven miniature golf course is Mount Sinai.

"I think it's a fun way to kind of go through the different stories of the Bible," she said. "I'm typically not a very religious person, but I think it's sweet."

In 1987, Tom and Sally Christopher bought the ice center and had a revelation to build the course. Sally said, "I think it was a God thing."

Tom, an accountant, had been handling the finances for the center. He knew it was not making much money but did not want to see it go out of business when the owner decided he wanted out. The center did fine in the winter, but Tom knew it needed something to bring in revenue in the warmer months of the year. He and his wife became true believers that a miniature golf course could save the struggling ice center and maybe a few souls.

Tom said, "If God can use an accountant and a housewife, He can use anybody."

The couple sat down at their kitchen table and, over the course of several months, designed a miniature golf course, using the Bible to shape the blueprints. It took them a year to fully plan the Old and New Testament courses that guide golfers through the Bible, from the Creation to the resurrection of Jesus. In 1991, they added the Miracles Course.

Sally said she would sketch a suggested layout for various holes and make cardboard models. "As we were drawing, Tom would say what we could or couldn't do construction-wise. We would think about it, pray about it, and make decisions."

Tom did most of the work himself, from pouring concrete to building waterfalls. Sally handled the landscaping. Now golfers come by the multitudes to have a whale of a time (just like Jonah) getting past such obstacles as a burning bush or lion's den.

Sally said she loves to watch players who want to understand the inspiration for each hole, such as the story in Exodus, where Moses puts his staff in the Nile River and turns the water into blood. That hole is covered in carpet that goes from blue to red. "I've seen a little child saying, 'This is the river, this is the blood.' You know, jumping back and forth, getting into the story," she said.

There is a sign at each hole describing the scene and the scripture that inspired it. For example, hole 7 on the Miracles Course is titled "An Ax Head Floats." Tom said a lot of people aren't familiar with that story that comes from 2 Kings 6:5–6: "Under the mighty hand of God, the prophet Elisha rescued an ax head from sinking in the Jordan River. By cutting a stick and throwing it in the same location, the ax head floated." To get the best score, golfers need to purposely hit their balls into a stream. Then the balls are pushed by the water to a landing just at the lip of the hole. That is just one of the many clever designs.

Golfers also pass through Noah's Ark, maneuver past a plague of frogs, and putt-putt through the tomb of Jesus, where Christian rock music plays through a speaker. Golfers say the homemade nature of it is a large part of the course's appeal.

Most of the course is a leisurely stroll through the scriptures, but it takes amazing grace to get past one cone-shaped hole that is labeled "Mount Sinai."

"I've seen a few people lose their religion over that hole," Tom laughed. "One man I can remember specifically on that hole said, 'I'm about to cuss, but I'm going to hold it back.' We weren't busy that day, so we let him keep trying, and it took him 139 strokes before he got in Mount Sinai!"

Tom purposely designed the course with an equal number of challenging holes and easy ones. For example, it takes just a gentle tap to get a hole in one on the "Seventh Day of Creation" green. That is because that is the day God rested.

The Christophers say Fairway to Heaven is not a big moneymaker, but it brings in enough to keep the ice center open in the summer, and it fits with their mission statement of running a family-friendly operation. Business really picked up in 2019, when the Travel Channel listed it as one of the Top Ten Most Unique miniature golf courses in the country.

Just like in life, golfers here find it is best to avoid obstacles and stay on the straight and narrow path. The designers want visitors to see this as a fun course and are delighted that for many people, it is also a biblical refresher course.

APPLE VALLEY HILLBILLY GARDEN AND TOYLAND

CALVERT CITY

If you are driving down U.S. Route 68 in Marshall County, there is a sign advertising a rest stop. That stop is a moldy couch by the side of the road. It is one piece of trash on a four-acre plot full of junk—a roadside attraction known as Apple Valley Hillbilly Garden and Toyland.

Stop, and in a manner of minutes, you are likely to be greeted by the Chief Hillbilly in Charge, owner Keith Holt. He proudly emerges from his home to give tours of his garden where bad puns grow like weeds.

A tree has a face with a toilet seat for lips. He calls it "Potty Mouth." A ditch full of old shoes is called the "Valley of Lost Soles." A circle of commodes is labeled "Thronehenge." You get the idea.

"When I travel, I always go to places like this," Holt said, gleefully. "I never thought I'd own a place like this."

After living in Los Angeles for twenty years, Holt moved his family back to his grandparents' land in 2005. He admits he is a pack rat, and his treasured trash soon piled up in the yard and woods around his house. One night, the sheriff showed up and told him he could not leave abandoned vehicles or appliances on the property.

"Well," Holt said, 'I asked him if it would be okay if it was turned into art. He said, 'I guess so,' so that's what I did."

He painted clowns on a trailer and hung bottles in trees. Soon, critics began to identify him as a folk artist. "I went from being a public nuisance to a local landmark!" Holt said. Now there is a sign at the entrance to his driveway that reads, "Sorry. We're Open."

Keith Holt, a master of bad puns, tells visitors that he "picked up a hammer and saw a tree with a potty mouth" while exploring his Hillbilly Garden. DIANNE KARNES

Neighbors have learned that if they have something the landfill won't take, they can take it to Hillbilly Garden. Holt has a scrapyard full of wires and tires, old tools, and broken electronic devices waiting to be turned into one of his eye-rolling creations.

"Actually, a plumber brought me eight toilets at once, and it was like Christmas to me," he laughed.

He has a forest full of "genuine, artificial Christmas trees." A stack of pans and skillets makes up his "pot patch." The trees in one section of his yard are always in "bud," with Budweiser cans hanging from the branches. You'll have a tough time keeping up with him as he leads you down his punny paths, talking a mile a minute. As you take it all in, you may feel like a deer stuck in the headlights. (He has a display like that, too.)

Most of the quirky construction really is just a collection of junk, but visitors are surprised when they go into a shed dubbed "Toyland." More than three thousand toys are shelved floor to ceiling, many of them with moving parts. He has playthings from the early 1900s to the present.

Many of these items are anything but junk. They have real value and are of museum quality. You can see vinyl figures of classic cartoon characters, plastic animals, antique dolls, and vintage lunch boxes.

Holt said the display in that shed is a shadow of what he envisions his Toyland to be. He has more than twelve thousand more toys, many of them stored in that trailer covered with clown paintings. He said he "collected toys like crazy" when he lived in Los Angeles, hitting up yard sales and flea markets and digging through dumpsters. Now he just needs money to build a proper exhibit hall to put everything on display.

"I want to create something everyone can come and enjoy," he said. "I want this to be a place where people relive their childhood."

Some people have called the whole toy exhibit one giant piece of folk art.

"We get visitors from all over the world," he said. Five people from China had toured the garden the week before I was there in 2019. He doesn't charge admission but does accept donations.

Holt's grandfather opened a small diner and gas station on the property when Highway 68 was paved in the late 1930s and later added a petting zoo. So the property has come full circle as a roadside attraction.

When Holt lived in Los Angeles, he had hoped for a career as an entertainer. He worked on movie sets and got a few acting jobs. To supplement his income, he built model train layouts for wealthy families. But now he is the star of his own show, nearly two thousand miles from Hollywood, on the family funny farm in Kentucky.

MORE TO EXPLORE

Kentucky has some amazing museums. In the state's largest city, you can spend hours at the Louisville Slugger Museum, the Speed Art Museum, or the Kentucky Derby Museum. There is no better place to explore the state's past than at the Thomas D. Clark Center for Kentucky History in Frankfort. Other standouts are the National Corvette Museum in Bowling Green, the National Quilt Museum in Paducah, and the Kentucky Folk Art Center in Morehead.

But for this series, I like to visit some lesser-known museums. One that gets very few visitors is the freaky and fascinating **Monroe Moosnick Medical and Scientific Museum** at Transylvania University in Lexington.

An immense hair ball is one of the many bizarre items on display at the Monroe Moosnick Medical and Scientific Museum.

Dr. Jamie Day, a physics professor, is the curator of a strange collection in the basement of the school's science building.

"I've only had two people faint," Day said when talking about visitors who have made appointments to see the museum.

It is easy to understand how one would feel queasy among the artifacts. The museum has a table filled with infant skeletons and loose bones. Another table holds a rare "Medical Venus," a life-size wax figure used to teach anatomy. It was made in Italy in the early 1800s with the organs modeled from the cadavers of two hundred women. The model was important because it kept students from robbing graves to study cadavers.

The university had a medical school from 1799 to 1859 that closed after many faculty members moved to bigger schools as the country headed toward the Civil War. "Because most of our artifacts survived, we have a more comprehensive medical collection than just about any school in the country for the time period," Day said. "Harvard has a bigger one, but many people say Transylvania has the second-best collection for teaching science from the early 1800s."

Some of the tools in the collection could be considered quackery, such as a device for blowing smoke into the bowels of drowning victims to revive them.

The most bizarre item in the museum may be a fourteen-inch hair ball that was cut from a cow's stomach in 1848, donated by Abraham Lincoln's brother-in-law. The hair ball even has its own X account (@ImmenseHairball). A lot of visitors also come to see a jar of a fleshy substance that fell from the sky in Bath County in 1876 in an event known as the "Great Kentucky Meat Shower." The most widely accepted explanation is that the meat was vomited by vultures flying overhead.

Those odd items draw visitors who seek out the stranger things in life. One of them was rocker Ozzy Osbourne, who came with his son, Jack, in 2018 to tape a segment for his reality show.

For now, the museum is open only by appointment and mostly to artists and researchers. Day hopes the university will someday be able to build a state-of-the-art exhibit hall for the collection and staff the museum for regular visiting hours.

Another bizarre collection can be found in Somerset at the **International Paranormal Museum and Research Center**. Co-owner Kyle Kadel has filled two rooms in the basement of the Carnegie Community Arts Center with items related to ghosts, aliens, voodoo, and cryptids.

The museum holds plaster casts professed to be Bigfoot prints, models of Moth Man, and dolls that are said to be cursed. Kadel has collected the items over the past fifteen years.

"The freakiest piece we have and, so far, the only piece I've not even wanted to touch is a voodoo doll," Kadel said. "It's one hundred years old and filled with grave dirt and human teeth."

There is also a "haunted" mannequin that once stood in a local department store. Former employees often said that when they reported for work in the morning, they would find that the mannequin had changed locations on the floor overnight when the building was empty. Kadel said several visitors to the museum have purported that it winked at them.

The building itself is claimed to be haunted. Kadel said a little boy died there in the early 1900s, and visitors have said they have heard him laughing.

"I love having a haunted museum," he said. "But I would not want to live in a haunted house."

He said even skeptics love the museum because it is preserving cultural traditions.

Fans of such curious and creepy collections can get a "twofer" by also visiting the nearby Paranormal Roadtripper's Nightmare Gallery.

Little things make a big impression at the **Great American Dollhouse Museum** in Danville. More than two hundred dollhouses are on display, but it is what is inside the houses that is truly amazing—tiny rooms with tiny people, staged in great detail by curator Lori Kagan-Moore.

She said, "It's a place where it's fair and safe and legal and fun to look in windows and see what people are doing."

It is also notable that the museum is not the result of a lifetime of collecting. In 2002, Kagan-Moore rediscovered a small dollhouse she had as a child and fell in love with it all over again. Everything in the museum has been bought or donated since 2005.

The real fun for the curator has been inventing stories to go with the houses. You will see movie stars in dressing rooms, children looking into sweetshop windows, and a bride who is late for her wedding. A visitor favorite is a house that allows you to follow a path of destruction from room to room by a boy who has been left home alone.

Many of the exhibits have a historical focus, set up to resemble life in the early 1900s, so a visit to the museum can be educational. But there are also displays that are just for fun, such as a fairy land and a cave full of dragons and trolls.

Kagan-Moore says the biggest misconception is that the museum is a place full of toy dolls. She said men and boys enjoy visiting just as much as women and girls when they see it is more about storytelling and craftsmanship. She hopes all visitors leave "feeling really happy" and a little sentimental.

$\sim$

Pioneer Playhouse, also in Danville, is not a museum, but it does hold a lot of history. It has been one family's labor of love since 1950.

Eben Henson returned to his hometown to start the theater when he was in his twenties after studying acting in New York. He took drama classes and made connections through the GI Bill after serving in the United States Navy in World War II.

His daughter, Heather Henson, said, "Some of his classmates were Tony Curtis, Bea Arthur, and Harry Belafonte, so he rubbed shoulders with some up-and-coming people."

Over the years, some actors on the rise performed on the outdoor stage Henson built in Danville, such as Lee Majors, Jim Varney, and a teenaged John Travolta. It is a summer stock playhouse that attracts professional actors from all over the country, and they live and work there for a season. Many return for multiple seasons.

Just before Eben Henson died in 2004, his family had many discussions about whether the theater would die with him. Son Robby Henson said, "When he was getting ill at the end, Dad said, 'It's so much work. I don't know if you kids want to do it.' But we do want to do it and continue what he started."

So Robby, a filmmaker, moved back from Los Angeles to be the artistic director. Daughter Holly, a standup comedian, moved back from Minnesota to be the manager, a role she filled for eight years before losing a battle with breast cancer. Now Heather is the manager. A second son, Eben Davis, is a traveling jazz musician and returns to help when he can. None of the Hensons are surprised to find themselves back where they grew up.

"I kind of feel like I grew up in a magical world," Heather said.

When I visited in 2022, their mother, Charlotte Henson, was still involved, too. At age ninety-one, she was singing folk songs to the crowds that came early for the buffet-style dinners that preceded the shows.

The playhouse still has steady attendance for the three shows it produces each summer, largely farcical comedies, and the family has no plans to retire the business.

"It's not Lincoln Center or Carnegie Hall," Robby said. "It's a very Kentucky theater under the stars. Audiences really engage with that and tend to come back."

If you love art, you can experience it in the great outdoors at **Josephine Sculpture Park** for free. More than sixty pieces of art are scattered among the weeds and woodland on this twenty-acre farm near Frankfort. Founder Melanie VanHouten sees it as her life's work to put more art into the world.

"It feels really comfortable being out in nature in a park setting," she said. "It's a lot more comfortable in a lot of ways than going into the white walls of a museum."

VanHouten was a sculptor for ten years in Minneapolis before returning to open this park on her grandparents' farm in 2009. It is named in honor of her grandmother, Josephine VanHouten.

This is not like a sculpture garden you may find in large cities. It has no formal gardens or concrete walkways. Instead, visitors walk dirt paths or cross through a field to see pieces of twisted metal sprouting from land that once grew tobacco or whimsical creatures that gather where cattle once grazed.

Donors and grants help pay for the art and upkeep of the park. Many of the pieces are on loan and may be on display for only a season. VanHouten said the park will never have a finished look, and that is just how she wants it. She said, "This is an ever-changing place where art meets the land."

⟡

A great day trip for shutterbugs is to map out a route through Fleming County, the **Covered Bridge Capital of Kentucky**. The state once had more than four hundred covered bridges, but just eleven are still standing. Three of them are in Fleming County. You can learn a lot about these picturesque pieces of the past at the Covered Bridge Museum in Flemingsburg, which is a good place to start your tour.

"It's amazing. People don't think about why they're covered," said museum director Brenda Plummer. "We get that question a lot." The answer is simple. There was no concrete or steel when the bridges were built in the early to mid-1800s. So the roof was to protect the wooden deck from decay. The bridges were also a place for travelers on horseback to get in out of the rain.

Ginny Reeves, vice president of the Fleming County Covered Bridge Authority, said a national preservation society determined that the Goddard White Bridge south of Flemingsburg is the second-most-photographed covered bridge in the nation, just behind one in Philippi, West Virginia. It has been featured in hundreds of books, magazines, commercials, and movies. It is so attractive because you can stand on one side of the creek and use the bridge to perfectly frame a quaint country church on the other side.

The other two bridges still standing in the county are the Grange City Bridge and Ringo's Mill Bridge in Hillsboro. Tourism could be what saves these structures, with folks in the county hoping people who come for the covered bridges will uncover other reasons to make a return visit.

Plummer said, "We try hard to make sure they're presentable and that when people come to visit, they go away with a good feeling."

꒜

Nostalgia is always on the menu at the last **Druther's Restaurant** in Campbellsville, and the dining room is never empty. The fast-food chain had a cult-like following in Kentucky and other southern states in the 1980s. It started as Burger Queen in Winter Haven, Florida, in 1956.

In 1981, the chain, which by then was based in Louisville, announced it was changing its name to Druther's, wanting to emphasize it had more than burgers. The name implied that you could go to other fast-food restaurants but that you would "druther" go someplace a little different.

By the early 1990s, Druther's was taken over by Dairy Queen. But because Campbellsville already had a Dairy Queen close by, the restaurant there was left out of the buyout. Current owner Steve McCarty said his father, who managed the franchise then, went out on his own and kept the name and the menu—a move that proved to be ingenious.

"A lot of the food is the exact same food we had all along," McCarty said. "The turnovers and onion rings taste the same."

It is not uncommon now to see people snapping pictures inside and outside the restaurant or to see license plates from far-off places in the parking lot. People make road trips to relive a taste of their youth. Facebook messages and YouTube videos show how many people have fond memories of the salad bar, the all-day breakfast menu, and the mascot, Andy Dandytale.

McCarty said one day, a visitor came in from the state of Washington and told him, "My buddy just got married in Lexington. As soon as I found out I was coming to Kentucky, I knew I was going to make a side trip to Druther's."

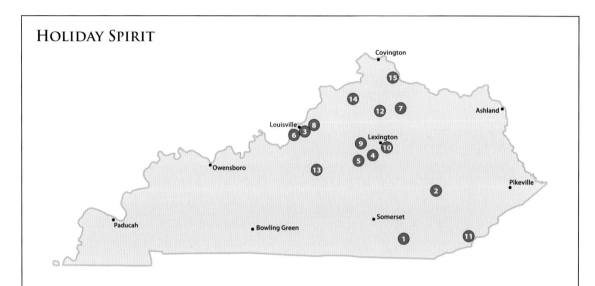

HOLIDAY SPIRIT

1. The Boy Who Loves Presidents, *Corbin*
2. Abe Lincoln Rock, *Owsley County*
3. Lovers Lane, *Louisville*
4. Lawn Mower Brigade, *Wilmore*
5. The Lady Who Danced Herself to Death, *Harrodsburg*
6. The Witches' Tree, *Louisville*
7. Courthouse Ghost, *Cynthiana*
8. Pope Lick Monster, *Jefferson County*
9. Anderson Hotel, *Lawrenceburg*
10. Unseen Lights, *Lexington*
11. Mountain Santa, *Harlan County*
12. Santa's Recording Studio, *Cynthiana*
13. Tree for Travelers, *Nelson County*
14. Bethlehem Post Office, *Henry County*
15. Stable Tradition, *Butler*

THE BOY WHO LOVES PRESIDENTS

PRESIDENTS' DAY

Corbin

Reed Elliotte with former president Jimmy Carter and First Lady Rosalyn Carter. LARRIETTA ELLIOTTE

Eleven-year-old Reed Elliotte spends a lot of time doing research in his Presidential Museum and Library. It is really his bedroom, but good luck finding the bed.

Every nook and cranny of his room is filled with presidential memorabilia—bobbleheads, blankets, plates, and posters. The fifth grader is a walking encyclopedia of White House wisdom.

Ask him to recite some odd facts about presidents, and he'll rattle off little-known tidbits:

"William Taft got stuck in the bathtub."

"John Quincy Adams swam naked in the Potomac River."

"Warren Harding had the longest feet of all presidents."

Reed met former president Bill Clinton during a volunteer project for a food bank in Nashville in 2023. LARRIETTA ELLIOTTE

Reed became fascinated with presidential history in 2018, when, at age seven, he watched television coverage of the death of George H. W. Bush.

His mother, Larrietta Elliotte, said, "Something just clicked in him, and he became immediately obsessed." She posted a picture of Reed saluting the TV during Bush's funeral procession, it got widely shared, and he became known as the "Boy Who Loves Presidents." All politicians, really.

"I've met Jimmy Carter, Vice President Mike Pence, Senator Mitch McConnell, Governor Andy Beshear, and so many more," he said. (After this story aired, he also met former presidents Bill Clinton and George W. Bush).

Reed is photographed with the politicians he meets, and he usually wears a red, white, and blue, stars-and-stripes suit. He is on his second one "because I outgrew the other one," he laughed.

People who meet Reed should be prepared for a takedown if he challenges them to a presidential trivia contest. Here is a transcript of my short-lived effort to stump him during a visit to his home in 2022:

Marvin:	*"Who was the first president to appear on TV?"*
Reed:	*"Franklin Roosevelt."*
Marvin:	*"That's right! When was Alexander Hamilton president?"*
Reed:	*"He wasn't a president."* (My trick question backfired.)
Marvin:	*"You ask me one."*
Reed:	*"Which president's father was a blacksmith?"*
Marvin (after a long delay):	*"Abe Lincoln?"*
Reed:	*"No, Herbert Hoover."*

To see this bright kid today, you would never know of the dark days in his past. A complicated birth damaged his kidneys, and he had to have a transplant at age two. His dad, Bill Elliotte, was the donor. Then Reed had two bouts with cancer, spending three months in the Cincinnati Children's Hospital for chemotherapy treatments when he was six years old. The lymphoma returned a year later, and doctors removed a tumor from his lungs. Reed was told to expect another long hospital stay and more chemotherapy, but that hasn't happened. Follow-up appointments have shown him to be cancer free. His family considers that a God-given miracle.

"I just trust the Lord to help me," Reed said.

Reed's family is delighted that he has a presidential fascination to keep him focused on the future. "I have joked for several years that I have had to give up my beach trips for presidential trips, but they've been some of the best family vacations we've had," his mother said.

They have traveled to several presidential libraries, the White House, and Mount Rushmore. They even attended church with Jimmy Carter in Plains, Georgia. Reed also appeared on *The Ellen DeGeneres Show*, demonstrating his monumental presidential knowledge to a national TV audience.

Reed has other obsessions, too, such as a love for country music and Loretta Lynn. He said he would have married her in an instant despite a seventy-nine-year age difference. He can sing most of her songs by memory.

Reed met former president George W. Bush and First Lady Laura Bush during a visit to Dallas in 2022.

What does he want to be when he grows up? President, of course, in 2048—the first time he would be eligible to run.

"I just want to get Democrats and Republicans to come together," he said. "We're just divided, and that disappoints me."

A lot of people have already told Reed he has their support when the time comes. Until then, he will keep "Biden" his time and thinkin' like Lincoln. Before my visit ended, he sat down at the piano to play a song for me. It was, of course, "Hail to the Chief."

ABE LINCOLN ROCK

PRESIDENTS' DAY

Owsley County

Abraham Lincoln is memorialized all over Kentucky, from statues in the capitol rotunda to college campuses, public squares, and riverside parks. Every school kid knows that the sixteenth president was born in a log cabin near Hodgenville. You don't have to go far to find his likeness on a pedestal, his face painted on a wall, or his name on a street sign. But one tribute is off the beaten path in rural Owsley County—way off the beaten path.

It takes a hike up an Owsley County mountain to see a life-size image of Abraham Lincoln carved in sandstone.

If you're lucky, the nine-year-old boy who lives at the base of the mountain will take you there.

Walker Gibson likes to see how visitors react when they see a life-size image of Abraham Lincoln carved into a boulder, five hundred feet up a mountain covered in kudzu vines.

"They're just amazed," he said. "Whenever there's really nothing to do, I just walk up here."

The sandstone sculpture was created sometime in the 1930s. There is some information about it on file in the local history section of the county library in Booneville.

Here is what is known. A peddler named Granville Johnson was working in the area when he became ill. A local family took him in, and he stayed with them for months. Often, the stranger would disappear into the woods for hours, and no one realized he was carving his masterpiece. After he moved on, the family discovered the carving of Lincoln. It is believed he left it as a thank-you gift for his hosts, who may have doubted his claims that he had been trained by an Italian sculptor.

"I think he might've just wanted to show them he knew something about sculpting. So it may have been a tribute, but it may also have been to prove a point that, 'Hey, I can sculpt,'" said Sue Christian, director of the Owsley County Alliance for Recreation and Entertainment.

Christian said the county once discussed moving the rock to a more accessible place, but that proved to be a monumental task that would be too difficult and too expensive. She said officials were also worried they would damage the carving.

You must cross private property to get to the sculpture, but landowner Wayne Gibson, Walker's father, said the family is more than happy to allow it.

"I try to be good to people," he said. "That's the Christian thing to do. It's pretty neat to just have something historical like that behind your house."

The Gibsons plan to keep the pathway open as long as visitors refrain from vandalism and littering. So far, that has not been a problem.

Local folks who would like to bring more tourists to Owsley County believe Lincoln could be a solid attraction. Winter is the best time to hike to the rock. The trail becomes too overgrown with kudzu in the spring and summer.

When Christian saw it for the first time, she said she couldn't believe how big it was. It makes her wonder how Johnson was able to reach high enough to carve Lincoln's head.

"There are just so many questions," she said.

Local history lover Dedria Morgan, an antiques dealer, said she would love for more people to know about the rock.

"We may not be here to ever see it become what we want it to be, but we are excited to know there are children who study Abraham Lincoln and they're willing to take the hikes and show people," she said. She hopes more teachers will bring students to the rock for field trips. She would love to see a state park open around it, but the site's remoteness may prevent that.

The carving does have some notoriety among scholars. It is listed in the Smithsonian Art Museum's Inventories Catalog as an example of outdoor folk art.

The site's unofficial tour guide is always willing to lead the way for anyone able to climb the mountain. Walker Gibson said enthusiastically, "It's worth the walk."

We may never know the whole story behind the chiseled features off Kentucky Route 846, but that is okay with local folks, who are simply happy it is there. They like that there is a little mystery with their history.

Lincoln Rock is about eight miles south of Booneville. To get there, take State Route 11 to State Route 846 and turn left on Abraham Lincoln Trail. Park just past the house on the right of the road and walk five hundred feet up the mountain.

LOVERS LANE

VALENTINE'S DAY

Louisville

A Jefferson County home is full of symbols of a couple's love. Paintings, paper hearts, and bobbleheads all give a nod to their devotion to each other. But in 2001, that love spilled out onto the road that leads to their house.

Les Terwilleger decided to decorate the stub of a tree with markers, spelling out "I love Jean," using a heart symbol in place of the word "love."

"I took a picture and framed it and gave it to her for Christmas," he said. "She looked at it and said, 'What's this?' I said, 'That's your tree, but you have to go find it.'"

She did find the tree along the road and loved it. So did other people. Soon, another love sign popped up on a nearby tree—and another, and another, and another.

"It makes me happy," Jean said. "Whenever I spot a new one, it gives me a spark of joy!"

Now Springdale Road is better known as Lovers Lane. "We'll have to get Google Maps to rename it," Jean joked.

The last time they counted, the Terwillegers found more than 140 signs.

There is a story behind each one of the public displays of affection. Jean would like to know each one of those stories, so she started a Facebook page (*Lovers Lane KY*) where sweethearts can post pictures and recount their romantic reasons for hanging a sign. "It's the little stories that fill your heart," she said. "They're more precious than any gift you can get."

Passersby learn that "Michael Loves Britt," "Greg Loves Kristy," "Beth Loves Pam," and "Alivia Loves Unicorns." They see that "Travis and Mary"

Signs of affection line Springdale Road in Louisville, which has become known as "Lovers Lane."

celebrated twenty years as a couple and that "Dogmeat and Regina" have been together since 1989.

Now grandparents are getting in on the act, hanging signs in honor of their grandchildren. There have been signs posted to propose marriage. And there are telltale signs that sometimes love is fleeting or one-sided. Those are the signs that disappear just a few days after going up.

The trees are on the public right-of-way, and Les says city transportation officials have told him they have no problem with the signs as long as they are maintained. Neither does the property owner, whose land borders the road. Les tries to repair signs that get broken or unsightly and removes ones that get put up where they shouldn't be, such as on utility poles.

The Terwillegers say the movement shows no signs of slowing down. They challenge people to start Lovers Lanes in their own communities.

There have now been eight versions of the "I ♥ Jean" message that started it all. Time, vandals, and the elements took their toll on the earlier signs. The latest one is metal, surrounded by solar lights. As the couple admired the sign on a winter day in 2019, they stumbled on part of the original one on a rotting log.

"I'm going to take my chainsaw and take a piece of this back to our yard," Les said.

Les and Jean have enjoyed every step of their half century together, and some of the best steps have been on Lovers Lane.

LAWN MOWER BRIGADE

INDEPENDENCE DAY

Wilmore

(Groan Alert: This story has more puns than are normally allowed in a news report!)

Wilmore is the picture of a patriotic town. It may be small, but its annual Fourth of July parade has the same things you will see in big-city processions: police and politicians, cars and kids, and floats and flags.

But during the 2017 parade, one annual entry was missing. A group that practiced for hours to be in the lineup had to cancel because of the weather. Rainy days don't cut it for what it does.

The Wilmore Lawn Mower Brigade is a parade tradition that dates to 1992.

Asbury College music professor Lynn Cooper set the wheels in motion back then. In recent years, a pastor, Daryl Diddle, has taken over the handles. He jokingly describes what they do as "fine art."

"You have to have a push lawn mower, a good sense of humor, and a little coordination," Diddle said. He said a sense of humor is the most important of those qualifications. "The other two are iffy," he said. "We can provide the lawn mowers if they don't have one."

Make no mistake: They do have coordination as they move at a good clip on their home turf. I watched as the group practiced in the week leading up to Independence Day, not knowing rain would cancel their performance. Codirector Glen Flanigan shouted out the commands and taught the team the mower maneuvers.

Members of the Wilmore Lawn Mower Brigade practice their drills before the city's annual Fourth of July parade in 2017.

The pushers weave in and out in various patterns, such as a figure eight, and crisscross paths, as Flanigan uses a whistle to signal each routine.

"When I do a short tweet, that just means move forward," he said.

They march to music that comes from a single speaker pulled on a wagon by a John Deere tractor. It is often the only music in the parade.

Two guys, Doug Butler and Ken Reitz, have run in the same circles since it all began twenty-five years ago. They get the honorary spots at the front of the line.

"It's hard. We end up drenched in sweat by the time it's done," Reitz said. "But it's just fun to do, so I keep coming back."

Even though the brigade missed the parade, it got to perform for an audience. People watched from their porches as the lawn boys practiced on a neighborhood street in the days leading up to the parade. And, of course, like in past years, jokesters called out, asking if they would mow a few lawns while they were out.

"Absolutely," said Flanigan. "And they want to know why we didn't bring weed eaters."

The group varies in size. Some years, there may be a dozen people; other years, twice that many. Recruitment posters go around town each spring.

It was a tough call to sit out the parade, but wet streets and sharp machines don't mix. The drill team's absence stood out like a tall blade of glass.

Parade-goer Julie Jobryce said the parade just wasn't the same without the Lawn Mower Brigade, which always goes the extra yard to entertain the crowd. "But we'll look for it next year," she said.

Yes, there's always next year. You can bet the cut-ups will be out each summer, sharpening their skills and hoping for a sunny return to tradition on July 4.

THE LADY WHO DANCED HERSELF TO DEATH

HALLOWEEN

Harrodsburg

There's not much left of the Harrodsburg Springs Hotel—just remnants of a wall and a springhouse over a site where soothing mineral waters used to flow. But in the early to mid-1800s, it was a resort that attracted wealthy visitors from far and wide.

Local historian and antiques dealer Jerry Sampson said, "It was a huge place in its time. People would gather there typically from May to October to, what they called, 'partake in the waters.'"

Each year around Halloween, Sampson is asked to dust off a story tied to a grave on the grounds of the former resort, a grave marked "Unknown." It's the story of a woman who checked into the hotel around 1840. She came alone, claiming her father was a prominent judge who would be arriving later. An employee showed her to her room, where she stayed until the grand ballroom opened that evening.

"The music began to be tuned up," Sampson said. "Musicians rosined up their bows, and as soon as that first note struck, this beautiful young lady glided down the staircase and captivated everyone who was in her presence."

The story goes that the woman joined in the very first dance, then the second one, and the third, as men in the room lined up to capture her attention. Sampson, an excellent storyteller, said the woman danced every dance and told one of the men it was the happiest night of her life.

These illustrations imagine the ghost many people have claimed to see at the grave of the "Lady Who Danced Herself to Death" in Harrods-burg's Young's Park.

"And as that happy night was ending, sadness struck," Sampson said. The stranger collapsed into the arms of her partner and died on the ball-room floor.

As he tells it, "The hotel owners waited a week for someone to come to identify the body, but no one did. They searched her room, and the only thing that was in the small trunk was the dress she arrived in. No journal. No diary. No ledger. Nothing."

So the owners had her buried on the property near a large tree with a marker that commands respect. It reads, "Hallowed and Hushed be the place of the dead; step softly, bow head."

Years later, the ballroom burned, the mineral springs dried up, and the hotel became a military asylum after the Civil War.

Other fires followed and the whole place was pretty much forgotten by the mid-1900s, and so was the mysterious dancer—until one night when a woman who was walking near the grave site told friends she had encountered a ghostly figure.

"The figure approached her and said, 'Can you please help me? I was dancing at the Harrodsburg Springs, and I've lost my way,'" Sampson said. "And the woman said, 'Oh my dear, don't you know? Harrodsburg Springs burned to the ground more than a hundred years ago!'"

With that news, Sampson said the figure began weeping and disappeared. It was the apparition of the lady who danced herself to death decades ago. Since then, other people have reported seeing a ghost near the grave, which is on property now known as Young's Park. Those who have heard the story come looking for her on moonlit nights, hoping to get a glimpse of the mysterious lady, twirling under the trees to music only she can hear.

Historians now believe the grave may hold the body of Mollie Black, a woman who disappeared from Tazewell, Tennessee, around that time. But a stamp-collecting group recently found a letter with Mollie's name on it and a Confederate stamp, casting doubt on that theory. The Confederate States of America existed twenty years after Dancing Lady died. Some people believe the woman was murdered and have proposed exhuming the body for DNA testing. Jerry Sampson is not in favor of it. He believes Harrodsburg should hold on to its legend without trying to analyze it too much.

THE WITCHES' TREE

HALLOWEEN

Louisville

Old Louisville is a wonderful place to take a stroll under stately trees, but there is one tree that some people avoid. It is at the corner of 6th Street and Park Avenue and is known as the Witches' Tree.

"It's gnarled and twisted. It just looks like it has a story to tell," said David Dominé, an author and tour guide in the historic neighborhood.

He retells the legend of the tree each time he leads a walking tour.

Here is how it goes. There used to be a beautiful maple tree on that corner, where witches gathered to cast spells and mix potions. But in 1889, city

Beads and pendants hang from the gnarled tree that legend says sprang up in Old Louisville after a coven of witches put a curse on the city.

leaders in Louisville announced they would have the tree chopped down to use as a maypole for a spring celebration. The witches warned local leaders to leave the tree alone, but the officials cut it down anyway. As the tree fell, the witches scattered, cursing the city as they fled.

The next spring, as plans were being made for May Day, a terrible tornado hit the city. It leveled hundreds of homes and businesses and killed more than a hundred people. Dominé says many of the people who died were on the city's May Day planning committee.

The tornado is well documented. The Filson Historical Society calls it "one of the most violent and damaging storms in the city's history." Newspaper headlines from March 1890 called the tornado a "storm demon," and articles described how the streets were filled with long funeral processions for more than a week.

Legend has it that when the twister moved through the Park Avenue neighborhood, lightning struck the stump left behind when the maple tree was felled.

"There was a tremendous explosion, a shower of sparks and flames and smoke," Dominé said. "They say the tree you see there today magically sprang up from the earth to replace the one stolen from the witches. They say its current appearance is more appropriate for witches."

The hedge apple tree is ugly, with exposed roots and limbs covered with knots. From a distance, it looks as if it has warts.

You don't have to believe in magic and curses to enjoy a good story. People visit the tree today because they like surprises and never know what they are going to see there. Trinkets are scattered all around the trunk, and various charms and necklaces hang from the branches. You might also see dolls stuck into crevices, and you could find candles, bones, or miniature brooms.

"Over time, more and more people have realized you've got to leave something," Dominé said. "A lot of times before they go to the racetrack, they will leave a horseshoe. That's supposed to bring good luck. Or they'll tuck in coins or leave beads, especially after Mardi Gras."

The tree has become so well known that it even has a Facebook page (*The Witches' Tree*). Dominé says, with tongue in cheek, that it is maintained by modern-day witches who post spells against people who steal trinkets from the site.

"They're equal opportunity witches, though, because when people leave nice things, they'll give them a good-luck blessing." The page links to Dominé's website.

People who live in nearby apartments have become used to the traffic around the tree. It has a charmed life, and it is unlikely city officials will ever want this one to be removed.

"I wouldn't recommend cutting it down," Dominé said. "It didn't work out well the last time."

COURTHOUSE GHOST

HALLOWEEN

Cynthiana

If you need a clock fixed in Cynthiana, you go to Ewalt Jewelers. Steve Ewalt spends most afternoons trying to get pendulums to swing, bells to chime, and timepieces to tick. But his biggest job is across the street at the Harrison County Courthouse, maintaining the large clock in the tower.

"I just enjoy keeping it running," Ewalt said.

Steve Ewalt works on the antique mechanism that keeps the clock working in the tower of the Harrison County Courthouse, surrounded by walls covered with names and weather statistics recorded by former timekeepers.

He makes the climb up narrow steps and through a trapdoor only about four times a year just to put a little oil on the gears or adjust for time changes.

"I turned the clock on at the last time change in the spring, and it's still right on," he said in October 2021. "This thing is amazingly accurate."

Ewalt got the job in 2015, when the former clock keeper died. The only instructions are on a framed piece of paper on the wall. "Essentially, all that says is use ten-weight oil. So the rest of it I've figured out on my own."

The clock has been in place since the courthouse was built in 1851. It was weight driven then. Now it runs on electricity. It tolled away the hours during the Civil War and survived a raid by Confederate general John Hunt Morgan in 1864, when most of Cynthiana was burned to the ground.

"I've heard stories that soldiers hid up here in one of Morgan's raids," Ewalt said.

Union soldiers used the courthouse as a hospital, and it is believed they stored dead bodies in the clock tower. Some people believe one of the soldiers is still there, not knowing his time is up.

"I swear I heard it one night," Ewalt said.

He said he was in the tower before midnight to make the clock spring forward when he heard a door slam on the landing below.

"So I stopped to see if I could hear any footsteps, and there weren't any," he said. "I know I locked the front door behind me, and I can't imagine anyone else wanted to be in the building at that time. That sure got my full attention when I heard that door slam!"

The next morning, Ewalt told clerks at the courthouse what had happened, and they said, "Oh, that's just Luther. He moves things around all the time."

But, as the story goes, a ghost hunter explored the tower one night and contacted the spirit, who told him he was a soldier named Frederick, not Luther.

Previous timekeepers recorded their names and weather statistics on the walls of the tower, dating back to 1862. Ewalt signed his name there on his first night on the job, which was appropriately Halloween. He remembers looking through the vents on the exterior wall of the tower and watching children trick-or-treating on Main Street.

Ewalt is not sure what to think about the ghost stories, but if Frederick or Luther is still there, the clock keeper believes he is harmless. However, Ewalt does admit he now avoids working in the tower late at night by himself.

"When it's time for a time change, it happens about twelve hours too soon!" he said, laughing.

POPE LICK MONSTER

HALLOWEEN

Jefferson County

The Pope Lick Trestle near the Fisherville neighborhood in Jefferson County has been around since the late 1800s. It is a landmark that draws hikers and bikers to the paved trail that runs under it. It is also home to a dark legend, best told in the light of day.

"I like the idea that monsters lurk somewhere just outside the visual range and could possibly exist," said Rod Whitenack, who grew up in the area and now works for a company called Louisville Halloween. One of his jobs is to run a gift shop at Pope Lick Park and operate an outdoor escape

A large model of The Goat Man looms over visitors to the gift shop at Louisville's Pope Lick Park.

game there based on the legend of the Pope Lick Monster. The shop is full of items featuring the famous cryptid, including caps, T-shirts, toys, and books. It also features a huge statue of the monster, known as The Goat Man.

"We can trace the legend to at least the 1950s," Whitenack said.

According to the story, the creature is half man, half goat. It hides in the woods by day and hangs out on the trestle at night. If people go looking for him, he can hypnotize them with his red eyes, forcing them to walk out onto the tracks to be hit by a train.

Whitenack's version of the story identifies The Goat Man as a former sideshow attraction.

"He was found as an infant and treated as a freak. He lived in chains in the circus and was fed from the grease pits of the carnies and was treated miserably for years. So when he finally broke out, he hated humanity."

The legend says the circus train wrecked on the trestle, allowing The Goat Man to escape. He has never left the area.

Sadly, one part of the story is true. At least five people have died on the trestle, most recently a teenage girl who was hit by a train in 2019. There is a makeshift memorial set up for her under the bridge, with pictures, candles, and flowers. According to Louisville's *Courier Journal*, the boyfriend of a young woman from Ohio who was killed by a train in 2016 admitted they were there to look for the monster. He survived by hanging from the side of the structure.

The trestle is 742 feet long, with a ninety-foot drop at the center. There is no way to outrun a train if you get caught in the middle of the trestle when one comes along. It is illegal to go on the tracks, and Norfolk Southern Railroad will prosecute anyone caught trespassing. Several signs warn that the line is still active.

"We always try to tell everyone, 'Please, please stay away from the trestle.' If you want to see The Goat Man, come to one of our attractions, and we promise you, you will see The Goat Man," said Whitenack. An actor in a creepy costume will jump out at people looking for a scare when they play the escape game.

Another version of the legend is that The Goat Man will come down from the trestle on nights when there is a full moon. It is said he can run sixty miles per hour and often jumps on the hoods of cars of those who dare to drive under the elevated bridge.

"I've heard stories from people who say, 'He ripped off my car door hinge' or 'He chased me, and there were scratches on the side of my car.' Those are the stories I heard a lot when I was a kid," Whitenack said.

There was a real-life goat man who roamed the eastern United States in the mid-1900s. Ches McCartney of Georgia traveled in a wagon pulled by a herd of goats, and, according to Whitenack, he did camp at least one time in a field near the trestle, staying for several weeks. I found a *Courier Journal* article from October 5, 1953, that confirms McCartney was in Louisville. The article said hundreds of people had stopped by a vacant lot along Bardstown Road to see the traveling man and his train of twenty-seven goats.

"People would bring their families on the weekend and come see this guy, and he would sell postcards and pose for pictures," Whitenack said. "Many people thought he was weird, and he smelled funny because he lived with goats." He was also known to share sermons with anyone who would listen.

Many people believe McCartney's odd behavior likely inspired the legend. Whitenack said parents may have tried to scare their children away from danger by telling them to "stay away from the trestle, or The Goat Man will get you!"

Whatever the origin, the tale has grown into a Halloween story of monstrous proportions, an urban legend that many people believe is worth keeping alive.

Whitenack said, "I think it connects us to our culture, it connects us to where we live, and it just makes our lives more interesting."

ANDERSON HOTEL

HALLOWEEN

Lawrenceburg

The Anderson Hotel is covered with tarps and scaffolding, protecting people who are passing on the sidewalks from falling bricks and fixtures loosened by fierce winds in the spring of 2023—a storm that brought down the iconic neon sign that hung on the outside of the two-story building. But the real danger may be inside, where things have been unchanged since the 1980s.

The lobby is furnished with old sofas and fabric-covered rocking chairs. A console television sits along one wood-paneled wall, and an end table

The lobby of the Anderson Hotel looks just as it did when it closed in 1985.

holds a rotary phone. A shabby rug covers part of a linoleum floor. The whole place smells moldy. Caretaker Jeff Waldridge said the lobby and all the rooms are "like little time capsules of energy."

The hotel was built in 1935 but never lived up to its potential as a premier place to stay. Waldridge said during the Prohibition era, Anderson County's bourbon industry tanked, hurting the economy. It was folly to build a twenty-six room hotel in Lawrenceburg during the Great Depression. So it quickly went downhill and was turned into apartments in the 1950s.

Waldridge said the Anderson Hotel became a "flophouse" where drug addicts, ex-convicts, and prostitutes could rent a room for as little as $2 a day. "That would be the equivalent of a $30 room today, which is a terrible idea."

Everyone was evicted forty years ago.

"The lease agreement stated that if you didn't pay your rent, they would lock your door and keep your things," Waldridge said while walking down one of the building's hallways. "So there were a lot of personal items left here, and I think that lends to some of the hauntings."

Waldridge, who is fascinated by tales of ghosts and cryptids, got permission to do paranormal investigations in the hotel thirty years after it was shuttered. He said the building may be untouched, but visitors are not.

"We've had people bitten three times by human bite marks up here," he said. One of those encounters with unseen forces is supposedly documented in a 2016 episode of the television series *Paranormal Lockdown*. A camera operator shouts out that he feels he has been attacked. When he lifts his shirt, viewers see scratches on his skin and the outline of a bite mark. Waldridge was in the room during the taping and believes the attack was real.

Soon after that, the hotel was flooded with requests from ghost hunters. Others who came in also reported scratches or feeling invisible hands around their throats or tugging at their hair. The building's owner stopped allowing investigations in 2017, deeming it too dangerous. No one other than Waldridge went to the second floor again for several years.

Waldridge said he has documented that at least thirteen people died in the hotel, including three by suicide. A manager shot himself, a man hanged himself in a closet, and a woman slashed her wrists on a bed. As Waldridge was going through the building during an investigation, he found a bloody mattress stuffed down a back stairwell.

The building's owner trusts Waldridge and is once again allowing curious visitors to tour the old hotel in controlled conditions, with Waldridge as their guide. Recent guests have told of hearing footsteps, seeing shadow people, and seeing a burning man near a bed even though there are no reports that the hotel was ever on fire. Those things happen in the so-called bad side of the building, an area that Waldridge still keeps off-limits to most people. Only serious investigators go there.

"There is one ghost that people see—thank God, I've never seen it—that they call the legless man," Waldridge said. "He walks on his hands with no legs."

Hundreds of people went through the "less haunted" side of the building in October 2023, when the hotel was set up as a Halloween attraction, although Waldridge said there is no part of the hotel that is free of spirits. "Some of them know they are dead, and they use that power to mess with people," he said.

Many people chickened out before they got very far into the tour not only because of the jump scares and costumed characters but also because of a sense of dread they got just from being in the building. A white board near the entrance was dubbed the "early checkout" list. It had scores of slash marks on it by the attraction's closing night.

The haunted house was partially based on stories attached to the hotel and embellished with the tale of a killer clown. The building itself inspired that story line after Waldridge started finding clown figurines throughout the building, left behind in cabinets or drawers. "It's almost like they're giving us gifts," he said.

Waldridge said he has an agreement with the spirits. He believes they will protect him as long as he protects the building. There are no plans to change a thing.

"It will remain what it is for the time being, and, you know, I think the ghosts are happy about that."

UNSEEN LIGHTS

CHRISTMAS

Lexington

Ryan Jones loves Christmas. He gets up on his roof in mid-November, fearlessly stringing lights for his annual display. He will hang more than ten thousand of them.

"I also make my own extension cords," he said.

Light displays synchronized to music have become common, but Ryan's display is different because he never sees the finished product. He is legally blind.

Kayla and Ryan Jones stand outside the home he decorates each Christmas even though he is blind.

Ryan Jones creates a synchronized light show each Christmas despite being legally blind.

"I have light perception, so I can see light and dark areas," he said. "I can see flashes of light and shadows in some circumstances, but I can't see much more than that."

He works all year, programming the light show on his computer, matching it to his favorite holiday music. He can't see the screen, but a robotic voice built into the software reads to him. He describes his program as twenty-five channels of light on a grid. He must control what each channel does each second. He can't just glance at the overall picture as most of us would do, then grasp the mouse and drag the pointer to a selected area. He must consider each channel separately, frame by frame—a process that takes months.

"You can purchase predesigned sequences, but I prefer to do everything from scratch," he said.

Ryan keeps strings of light near his keyboard. If he darkens the room and gets close to the lights, he can tell if they are blinking when he wants them to.

His wife, Kayla, is his eyes.

"She knows what I want and helps make sure I get there if something's missing," he said.

His display is an example of patience and perseverance, with lights going up and coming down several times before Ryan gets it exactly right. He wraps cords around the columns on his porch, feeling the spacing to make sure he has enough lights to cover them from top to bottom.

Knowing that he is blind, one can't help but be a little nervous to see him walking across the roof, holding on to the gutter, and placing a star between two second-story windows.

By the first weekend of December, it is showtime. Everything comes together in a half-hour presentation featuring seven songs and narration from the Bible, which can be tuned in on a car radio. Ryan and Kayla love it when drivers slow down or park on the street to watch.

"I hope people take away the message of Christmas," Kayla said. "It's Jesus' birthday, and I really want people to take away that if you have any sort of disability or perceived limitation, you can still do absolutely anything you set your mind to."

"The truth is, I do wish I could see the whole thing together," Ryan said. "I have a picture in my mind of what I think it looks like, but it would be pretty neat to see what everyone else sees."

Ryan Jones may not be able to see, but those who drive by his house in December know he certainly has a lot of vision.

❧

The light display began in 2014 and has grown larger each year. The house is on Abbington Hill in Lexington. You can see videos of past shows and get updates on future ones by following the Jones Family Christmas Light and Music Show *on Facebook.*

MOUNTAIN SANTA

CHRISTMAS

Harlan County

A storage building on Santa Lane in Wallins Creek doesn't look special on the outside, but inside, it is stuffed floor to ceiling with thousands of wrapped toys. They have been collected all year to be distributed in some of the state's poorest communities, places where coal mining jobs have disappeared and nothing has taken their place.

Volunteers flock to the building every December to load the toys into trucks and vans that will be driven into narrow mountain coves known as

Volunteers hand gifts to a family living in a shed in Harlan County as Jason Saylor fills the role of "Mountain Santa," originated by Mike Howard in 1975.

"hollows" or "hollers," where a third of the people live in poverty. It has been happening every Christmas season since 1975.

April Galloway organizes the caravans and maps out their routes. Her instructions to volunteers are simple: "One present per child starting out," she tells them, "unless the Lord moves on you to give more. You'll know it."

Her father, Mike Howard, started making the deliveries three years before she was born. She and her two brothers have never known a Christmas without this convoy of joy. But when I was there in 2017, there was sadness, too. Howard had to watch the lineup form through a window at his home. He was too sick to mingle with the friends and strangers there to carry on the tradition he started.

"It's humbling to know he's loved this much," Galloway tells the throng of volunteers as she addresses them from the bed of a pickup. "I can't thank you enough."

She fights back tears as she tells them, "He would be out here if he could."

Howard, who is known to some people only as "Mountain Santa," was diagnosed with stage 4 lung cancer in the spring of 2017. His treatments stole all his energy by winter. One could only imagine how difficult it was for this quiet, humble man to miss the trip into the hollows, where he was the only Santa some children had ever seen.

His son, Jordan, put on the Santa suit to lead one caravan, and family friend Jason Saylor played St. Nick for another run. Neither pretends to fill Howard's boots.

"It's sad that Brother Mike ain't here," said Saylor. "We miss him and wish it was him out here."

Each year, a police siren notifies the mountain people when Santa has arrived in their communities. The trucks go slowly past each house where a child could be living. Sometimes, a child comes out of a dilapidated shed or a camper that serves as a home. A volunteer hands adults goodie bags filled with candy and an apple or orange. Children get toys donated by church and civic groups from across the state and out of state, too. There are also a few used bicycles that have been refurbished.

"Ho, ho, ho," Saylor shouted from the back of the lead pickup. "Merry Christmas. God bless you!" It is a continuous chant as the truck goes down one curvy two-lane road after another.

Mike Howard put on a Santa suit and delivered toys in Harlan County for more than forty Christmases. APRIL GALLOWAY

By the time the operation finished, "Mountain Santa" had led more than one hundred truckloads of toys into the mountains over three days.

"When we come home, we're empty," Galloway said. "We go until we give out."

John Jenkins, who was unemployed but looking for work, came out of a house to accept gifts for his children. He called the volunteers "lifesavers."

"It makes a huge difference to me," he said, "and a bigger difference to my kids. Without this, I wouldn't be able to do what I'm going to be able to do on Christmas morning."

From the start, the volunteers have seen this as more than a toy drive. It is a ministry, and sometimes the only thing people ask for is prayer. Many times during the long days, the gift givers will gather in a circle around a recipient, bow their heads, and ask the Lord "to love on them."

This all started when Howard was in his twenties. He dressed up as Santa when a local merchant asked him to pass out candy to shoppers. He enjoyed it so much that the next year he collected some toys and went out on his own, knowing there were a lot of needy people in his community. His efforts grew into an operation that now gives out nearly four thousand toys each year to children and seven thousand apples and oranges to adults. Local folks have many stories about Howard's selfless acts of kindness and faith in others. He was known to go to a grocery store and fill up a shopping cart with candy bars, chips, and fruit and wait by the register. He said he knew someone would come along and offer to help him pay for it, and he never had to wait long before someone did.

December 2017 was the first time in forty-two years that he missed putting on the red suit. But that wasn't all that defined the retired coal miner, who was the youngest of eleven children. People throughout Harlan County knew him as a man who did charitable deeds year-round. For years, he made weekly trips to a nursing home to visit people who had no family members, often bringing them fresh fruit or milkshakes. He was also a regular visitor to the county jail, where he went to pray and share his faith with inmates.

"I always said this world would be something to see if there were more people like him," said Galloway.

You don't need to ask people in Harlan County if Santa is real. They have seen him in action for decades.

⌇

Mike Howard died on January 7, 2018, at the age of sixty-five, just two weeks after volunteers carried out his mission. His wife of forty-one years, Barbara Howard, followed him in death just ten months later. The "Mountain Santa" tradition continues each year, led by their sons, Jordan and Michael Howard, and daughter, April Galloway, who say they don't know any other way to celebrate Christmas.

SANTA'S RECORDING STUDIO

CHRISTMAS

Cynthiana

Garry Uhles does things a little differently than most people. He doesn't put on a suit until he comes home from work. He also puts on some music and, within minutes, becomes a different person.

This pharmacy technician by day turns into Santa Claus by night.

"We got the suit, and I was so excited," he said. "I tried to think about what we could do, and really, with our current situation, you can't get out there." You see, Uhles wanted to spread Christmas cheer in 2020 during the

Each December, Viota and Garry Uhles turn their living room into a recording studio for Santa and Mrs. Claus.

height of the coronavirus pandemic when masking and lockdowns were common. But his wife, Viota, had an idea. If kids couldn't see Santa face-to-face, the couple could put him in the palm of their hands. His way into their homes would be through videos they could see on mobile phones.

In mid-November, the pair turns their living room into a video recording studio, complete with a large holiday-themed backdrop, featuring a fake fireplace and mantle adorned with garland and candles. A decorated tree sits in one corner. Santa's chair is in the center of the scene, next to an end table holding a glass of milk and a plate of cookies.

Each night, Garry, dressed as Santa, records personalized messages to children. Viota hits the start and stop button on her cell phone, mounted on a tripod. They set up a Facebook page to let people know about their desire to spread holiday joy this way. Nearly four hundred requests came in the first week.

When parents request a video, Garry asks them to give him a few details about their child's life, such as names of pets or best friends, as well as a few items on their wish list. The one thing he won't do is tell children they have been bad or are in danger of not getting any presents.

Many nights, the couple stays up until past midnight recording the messages.

Tiffany Workman of Bourbon County was one of the first parents to get a personalized message for her youngest children. She said they watched it over and over. Her son, Jace, was surprised Santa knew he had just turned four years old.

"The kids have had a really tough time this year as far as COVID goes," Workman said. "So bringing the magic back is probably one of the best things for a parent right now."

Viota didn't intend to be part of the videos. She organizes the requests and sends out the videos. But Garry wanted her to come out from the shadows and encouraged her to buy a "Mrs. Claus" costume. So she steps out from behind the camera during each video to deliver milk to Santa or add her own greeting to the children. She admits she enjoys it as much as her husband does.

"I'm a nurse, so my job is a little stressful, but when we come home and start doing these videos, everything else just melts away," she said.

Garry said making the videos just warms his heart. There is no charge for the service.

"The only payment I want is to see happy kids."

When watching Garry make the videos, it is easy to see why he always wanted a Santa suit. It fits him perfectly.

꒰

Garry and Viota Uhles have continued to record videos each Christmas season, although they do have to stop accepting requests by mid-December. They hate to say no to anyone, but with thousands of requests for personalized videos coming in, it is just not possible to get them all done. Their Facebook page is Santa Videos and Stories (GAU).

TREE FOR TRAVELERS

CHRISTMAS

Nelson County

Bardstown has a small-town charm that is well documented, and at Christmastime, the courthouse square and downtown shops are dressed in holiday style. The large tree in the roundabout is the center of attention. But it is another tree, three miles outside of town, that was at the center of a mystery for more than a decade.

Kim Huston, president of the Nelson County Economic Development Agency, said the tree is a frequent topic of conversation. "No one knew who put it up or when it went up," she said.

I found out.

The tree was first noticed in the summer of 2008, when someone decided to spruce up a cedar along the Bluegrass Parkway. Still today, its branches are trimmed in tinsel and full of bows, bells, and birds that swing in the breeze every time a car zooms past.

The sly guy behind the roadside attraction is Don Fulford, who now lives in Perryville, Missouri.

Back then, Fulford commuted to work early every weekday morning from Elizabethtown to Versailles. One morning, after a night of cleaning out his attic, he had some old ornaments in his car, destined for the dump. But the lone tree caught his eye. He stopped that morning and put the glass bulbs on the tree. He said that for over a month, he stopped almost every morning around 5 a.m. to add decorations to the tree; other things he could find around the house or pick up at dollar stores.

Ornaments hang from the lower branches of a cedar tree along the Bluegrass Parkway, which has been decorated for Christmas since 2008.

"It was pretty routine for me," Fulford said. "I'd pull over in that curve and walk on over. If somebody did come by, I'd just hide behind the tree until they passed."

Fulford said that as his clandestine operation went on, he remembered an old story about a man who left his troubles on a tree every night instead of taking them home with him. So he named the ornaments after problems such as stress and worry and left them by the side of the road.

"It's such a simple thing, but it lifted my spirits," he said. "I hope it inspires others."

Over the years, Fulford's sneakiness branched out to other people who wanted to make sure the tree sparkles year-round. He first learned he had helpers about a year after his ornaments went up.

"I'm driving (one day), and I look over, and there are presents and more garland and lights, and I just started smiling," he said. "I read a little later on that some wonderful people had decorated it for a friend who was dying of cancer and would probably never see Christmas again."

Now the tree often gets new decorations for Valentine's Day, Mother's Day, or the Fourth of July. Fulford says it is no longer his tree—it belongs to everybody. The tree has become a symbol of hope and, according to Bardstown's economic development director, a symbol of small-town charm.

"A Christmas tree at the entrance to town, whether it's Christmas or any other time of year, tells about the spirit we have in our community and the spirit that lives on," Huston said.

What would happen if road crews decided to clear the decorations off the tree or cut it down?

"They wouldn't dare," Huston said, laughing. "They know people would hunt them down!"

The tree was about six feet tall when Fulford first decorated it. It is now three times that size, and no one can reach high enough to put decorations in the top half.

"Never in a million years did I dream it would still be around years later," Fulford said. "I don't mind if that ends up being my legacy. It'll be okay."

He was reluctant to come forward and admit he was the original decorator because he liked that there was a sense of wonder and mystery surrounding the tree. But Fulford also realized that by telling his story, other people might be encouraged to do something that makes a connection with others.

"I hope someone sees the tree and says, 'You know what, I have a long time to be on this road. I'll give a call to someone I haven't talked to in a long time.'"

The tree has become a landmark at mile marker 18 on the northbound side of the Bluegrass Parkway. It causes weary travelers to look for glimpses of joy, even at seventy miles per hour.

BETHLEHEM POST OFFICE

CHRISTMAS

Henry County

The small community of Bethlehem, population 160, sees increased traffic each December as people find their way to its little post office.

In 1947, postmaster Anna Laura Peyton designed an image to be rubber-stamped on Christmas cards, depicting three wise men following a star. Paired with the Bethlehem postmark, it became a sought-after item. Peyton was postmaster for more than forty years, running the post office out of her home. She applied the stamped design in either black or red ink, depending on which would look best on the envelope.

Christmas cards mailed from Bethlehem, Kentucky, get a special stamp depicting three wise men on camels.

As the stamp grew in popularity, she found herself quite busy each December. Volunteers helped her add the image to the stacks of cards that came in from neighboring communities, across the state, and, eventually, around the world. Her granddaughter, Melinda Spear, was one of her helpers and said some years, the tiny post office handled more than one hundred thousand holiday cards.

The tradition continued when Spear's uncle, Cecil Peyton, took over from 1981 to 2001. There were other postmasters in the first part of the twenty-first century, and they continued applying the special postmark. In 2020, Spear became the postal clerk in Bethlehem, becoming the third generation of the same family to carry on the Christmas tradition. (The post office is now overseen by the postmaster in the Henry County seat of Eminence.)

The post office is now open just two hours each weekday and four hours on Saturday. Spear believes it is the Christmas postmark that has saved the post office from the chopping block at a time when so many small offices have been eliminated.

"December is my anchor month," she said. "It's the one that keeps us here for the year."

Fewer people send holiday cards these days, but Spear said she still expects to hand cancel about ten thousand cards with the Christmas stamp. She said she still gets them in from all over the United States as well as Great Britain, Scotland, Japan, and a few other countries. Many of the requests for cancellations come from collectors.

Cards come in large envelopes or boxes addressed to Bethlehem Post Office, 3946 Bethlehem Road, Bethlehem, Kentucky 40007.

Customers can send cards that already have postage on them, but Spear prefers when people leave them unstamped and include a check for the correct postage amount, made out to the Bethlehem Post Office. She said the revenue will help keep the office open.

Bethlehem also lives up to its name by staging a live nativity scene each year in an empty lot directly across from the post office. Actors and live farm animals fill the lot for two or three nights in the week leading up to Christmas. That tradition began in 1960, when the congregations of the local Baptist, Methodist and Christian churches joined forces to make sure there were enough volunteers to cover several shifts in the stable.

For the second time in this series, I decided to rhyme the story that was edited for television (see "Mother Goose Inn"). Here is the script:

> *Oh, Little Village of Bethlehem,*
> *How still we see thee lie.*
> *You can stand on the corner for quite a while,*
> *Before a single driver goes by.*
>
> *But one place, the post office, is busy,*
> *Each Christmas card gets an addition.*

Spear: *"My grandmother was the one who actually got it in here*
> *And started the tradition."*
>
> *In 1947,*
> *A special postmark was unfurled.*
> *It kind of put this place on the map.*

Spear: *"Because there are only eighteen Bethlehems in the world."*
>
> *The postmark shows the Magi,*
> *And has become a thing of worth.*

Spear: *"It's bringing in the fact of Christ being born . . .*
> *Just celebrating his birth."*
>
> *The special mark caught on, in Kentucky*
> *And the world throughout.*

Spear: *"It wasn't unusual back then to have*
> *Close to a hundred thousand cards go out."*
> *"Those days have, unfortunately, come and gone,"*
> *Said third-generation clerk, Melinda Spear.*

Spear: *"The month of December is my anchor month.*
> *That's the one that keeps it here for the year."*
>
> *For just two hours most days, this post office stays open.*
> *While others have closed, here they keep hopin'*
> *That an ink pad is enough to keep the register filled.*
> *So far, so good.*

Spear:	*"I'm really thrilled."*
	Melinda still expects to cancel ten thousand cards or so.
	People still find their way here for this symbol of long ago.
	When the wise men went to Bethlehem,
	They took camels and followed a star.
	Now it's a whole lot easier, Route 22 by car.
	She's making world connections,
	When the cards pass through her hands.
Spear:	*"I got some from England and actually got some from Japan."*
	So many foreign lands.
	For Melinda, the postmarks bring back memories
	Of helping here in her childhood.
Spear (demonstrating):	*"Now see if you've got the room,*
	You can really put them on there good."
	Oh, little village of Bethlehem,
	You give us a taste of heaven.
	You make your mark at Christmastime
	From zip code 40007.

STABLE TRADITION

CHRISTMAS

Butler

On the weekend before Christmas, the Kirsch family of Pendleton County gets together at their homeplace for dinner, devotions, and prayer. Then they get all dressed up to share their faith in a bigger way.

Brothers, sisters, grandchildren, nieces, and nephews put on robes, wings, or crowns in the farmhouse basement, which is also a costume closet, and then go away to a manger in a back field where cars are lined up to see a familiar scene take shape.

This all began in 1992, when Kenna Knight said her parents, Ken and Bonnie Kirsch, were talking to the family about what they could do to make the holiday special. "We decided the best way to bring the true meaning of Christmas into the season and keep that in the forefront was to start a live nativity," Knight said.

Everyone born into the family or married into it has been a part of it ever since. They take turns performing the distinct roles in the three-hour event in one-hour shifts. Almost every family member is there for the three nights of the live nativity. Those who aren't in the stable are greeting visitors, directing traffic, or passing out cookies and hot cocoa.

Nineteen-year-old Jordan Kirsch stood near the manger in 2022 wearing a royal-looking robe and holding a bag of "gold." "I've been an angel for a significant part of it, and now I got promoted to a Wise Lady!" she laughed.

The costumes are not just bath robes and scarves. They were designed and sewn together over the years by Bonnie's mother, Betty Bierman, who at

The Kirsch family nativity has been a tradition since 1992. Pictured, from left, in 2023: Moriah Conrad, Jessa Conrad, Bethani Kirsch, Cody Kirsch, Davis Conrad, Jordan Kirsch, Aaron Kirsch, and Gab Kirsch. JOSIE ARKENAU

102 years old was still part of the tradition. She stood ready to repair holes on a holy night.

"I don't make anything now," said Bierman. "But if somebody needs a seam sewed up or a patch, I keep my machine open."

A lot of people decorate with nativity scenes, made up of plastic figures or wooden cutouts, but this family believes a live scene is a better representation of the biblical stable. Their stable is full of visitors, noise, and joy, just as they believe the one in Bethlehem was when Christ was born.

"It's the ability to communicate and share that makes a live nativity scene better," said Knight. "We get to tell our story and why we do it, and we get to hear their story as to why they come."

This is not meant to be a drive-by experience. Visitors are encouraged to get out of their vehicles and interact with the actors and to pet the sheep, goats, cows and donkeys penned up outside the stable. Some years, they have rented a live camel to add to the display.

"We now have people who came when they were kids bringing their kids, and they will tell you how it's become a big part of their family traditions as well," said Knight.

Bonnie Kirsch died in July 2022, so the family said there is now a void in the event. "She loved it so much," said her son, Matthew Kirsch. "She's a big reason it has continued all these years. We'll keep it going as long as we can."

Bonnie's husband, Ken, agrees. "We have a pretty expanded family, and it keeps expanding, so I think it will go on for a while."

Eight-year-old Abby Insko has been coming to the live nativity scene for as long as she has been alive. "I like it because whenever I was three, I got to hold baby Jesus," said Abby. Her mother keeps a picture of that moment on her phone. The baby is always a doll. The family never wanted to expose a newborn to the elements of December.

Braden Wolfe of nearby Falmouth has also been a frequent visitor over the years. "It's awesome," he said. "A nice, small-town thing to do."

"I love it because I know we're serving the Lord, and I know we're touching a lot of people, and it's very important to me that that happens," Bierman said.

What started as a simple gift to the community has become a star attraction.

About one thousand people visit the scene each year, which is staged on the Friday, Saturday, and Sunday of the week before Christmas. Nativity weekend has never been canceled no matter how bad the weather has been. The farm also has a large light display that can be viewed every night from Thanksgiving to New Year's Eve at 35 Jacobs Road in Butler.

MORE TO CELEBRATE

Holidays are always good topics for a *Spirit of the Bluegrass* segment. There are some great traditions that are well known, such as **Southern Lights at the Kentucky Horse Park** and **Lights under Louisville**. Both of those events draw Christmas crowds by the tens of thousands.

There are countless pumpkin farms and corn mazes that delight children each fall, and the festivities leading up to the Kentucky Derby each May make that event seem like a holiday. All those events are visually pleasing and worthy of television coverage, which they receive on a regular basis. I try to seek out holiday stories that are not as common.

That is why I found Covington's **Garden of Hope** to be intriguing in the days before Easter. It is a small park that sits on a hill overlooking Interstate 75, created by the Reverend Morris Coers. The minister was inspired to build it after a visit to the Holy Land in 1938, wanting to let others experience a little of what he did in Israel. What he wanted most was to re-create the tomb of Jesus, something he finally did in 1958 using three hundred tons of concrete.

Coers died two years later but not before adding a replica of a carpenter's shop and a sixteenth-century Spanish chapel. Tourists used to come to the garden by busloads, and it has been a frequent site for weddings and Easter sunrise services. These days, unless you're lucky enough to find a caretaker on the property, you will find the tomb and the buildings locked. But visitors are still welcome to look around. Despite the noise of the interstate and some neglect, the original goal remains—to give people a place to pray and reflect on their faith.

⤳

I have always enjoyed ghost stories around Halloween. It is fun to play with the editing, making people transparent or shadows dance on walls and ceilings. With ghost stories, you don't have to confirm every statement is true or verify a place is haunted. That's not possible. You just get to tell a good tale.

It is easy to find scores of houses, theaters, and cemeteries that are said to be haunted. But it took a little research to discover that Kentucky has a different link to the paranormal. In 2017, I followed members of Bluegrass Ghost Chasers into the **Colville Covered Bridge** in Bourbon County.

At least three mysteries are tied to the bridge, which was built in 1877. Supposedly, a man hanged himself in the middle of the bridge a few years after it was built. And from the 1930s, there is the story of a young couple who came down the road after a dance. The man behind the wheel was driving too fast, missed the bridge, and plunged his car into Hinkston Creek, killing himself and his date. Another story centers on an elderly woman who was walking in the bridge and died of a heart attack before she made it through.

All three of those stories have played with imaginations over the years. Now visitors sometimes say they see strange shadows in the bridge, hear whispers, or see lights suddenly shine up through the floorboards as if coming from headlights in the water below. The ghost hunters didn't turn up any hard evidence that the bridge was haunted the night I was there, although members said the "air felt heavy," as if the bridge were cloaked in sadness.

⤳

Some people can single-handedly make a holiday happier. Although I wouldn't call Groundhog Day a real holiday, it is the best day of the year for Stacey Underhill of Lexington. She bought a groundhog costume in 2007 just because she thought it would be fun. She wore it while standing along a busy road on February 2, holding a "Happy Groundhog Day" sign, waving

Alter egos: Adam Allison as the Grinch and Stacey Underhill in her groundhog costume.

at cars and school buses. It was so much fun that she has done it every year since and hosts a party at her house with groundhog-themed snacks as the movie *Groundhog Day* plays in the background.

"People think I'm nuts," she said. But when it comes to spreading cheer, she casts a pretty long shadow.

Another Kentuckian who changes personality during a holiday is Adam Allison, the drama and music director at McNabb Middle School in Mount Sterling. On the last day of school before Christmas break, he shows up at school dressed as Dr. Seuss's Grinch. On this day, he makes mischief throughout the school, interrupting classes, jumping out from behind lockers to scare students, and leading the middle schoolers in boisterous songs and dances.

Allison learned how to make the transformation to the Grinch while working for ten years in Los Angeles in the entertainment industry. A former girlfriend showed him how to work with prosthetics and apply theatrical makeup. It takes him six hours to make the full transformation, which means he gets up at 2 a.m. to prepare for the last day of the semester.

His message to students is simple: "Express yourself!" One student told me Allison just knows how to make students enjoy coming to class. "He's like that all the time," said sixth grader Hannah Chase. "The first day of school, he jumped up on a table!"

Allison ended the last school day of 2018 chasing children onto their school buses, yelling "Merry Christmas!" It was as if the Grinch's heart had grown three sizes that day.

In 2023, I came across a Facebook post from two German visitors who were visiting Kentucky to tour the Bourbon Trail. Patrick Heining and Benjamin Fippl said that while they were visiting distilleries, they kept hearing about Thanksgiving and came to believe it was something they needed to experience American style. The more they heard about the feasts and the traditions, the more they realized they didn't want to eat in a fast-food restaurant on the fourth Thursday in November.

The travel partners boldly asked on the *Kentucky Road Trips* site if anybody would like to show a couple of German guys what Thanksgiving is all about. "We didn't expect much," Fippl said. "Actually, we were just doing it for fun."

But they didn't know about southern hospitality. Thirty invitations came in on the first day the plea was posted. One that really appealed to the tourists came from Leon Claywell, a retired pharmacist in Bardstown. He invited the strangers to spend the day with his family at his daughter's house in Nelson County, saying there is always room at their table. In past years, the Claywells had hosted visitors from England, Croatia, and Zimbabwe.

So Heining and Fippl nervously rolled up to the home of J. T. and Alyson Roby and found themselves instantly greeted by more than thirty people. They stayed the entire day, soaking up enjoyable conversation, sampling bourbon, and eating dozens of dishes they had never tried before, such as smoked turkey, corn pudding, green bean casserole, and pecan pie.

A simple Facebook post turned into an unforgettable cultural experience. The last-minute guests went away saying they were filled not only with food but also with love for newfound friends who told them to come back next year for seconds.

⌃

Most people love Christmas, but some people *love* it in a gigantic way. They *love, love, love* it! You can't use enough exclamation points or superlatives to describe their holiday spirit.

Spirit of the Bluegrass often gives a shout-out to the Christmas Overachievers, a term of respect for people who go all out for the holiday. One such person is Zach Neilson of Nicholasville. He programmed his first Christmas light display at his home when he was just ten years old.

"I went to an engineering camp, and it just sparked something," Neilson said. So as a preteen, he bought some software and taught himself how to connect lights to an audio track and lit up his family's home in a way it had never been decorated before. By the next Christmas, his hobby had spilled into the yard, up on the rooftop, and into his neighbors' yards in a display using more than twenty thousand lights and a hundred extension cords. That was the start of a flashy presentation that grew each year until he graduated from high school. Neilson's parents financed the project, buying lights and paying the electric bill, but the labor was all his.

His annual show, which caused traffic jams on Bernie Trail, was promoted as "Wild Lights." Each year, Neilson's displays included a donation bin to support charities he likes, such as local food pantries. He loves it when he goes somewhere and is still referred to as "Mr. Christmas."

Another die-hard decorator is Mary Lou Bohannon of Versailles. She puts up 110 Christmas trees in her home—in corners, on cabinets, in bedrooms, and in bathrooms. Her indoor forest is made up of trees of all colors, sizes, and many themes, such as farm life, Disney characters, or the Kentucky Derby. She said the most important tree is the first one guests see when they enter the front door, filled with symbols of both the birth and the resurrection of Jesus.

Bohannon moved to Woodford County from Shelby County in 2015 after her husband, Jerry, died, and she decided the house felt empty. "So I started doing all the trees and having people in my house. That's what made it a home and added some love to it," she said.

An above-and-beyond award should also go to Johnny and Shirley Richie of Lexington. Their home on Toronto Road in Lexington is known as the "Inflatables House." Their small yard is crammed full of inflatables at Christmas as well as Halloween, Valentine's Day, Easter, and Independence Day. Johnny believes he has about four hundred inflatables, but he has lost count.

The Richies love it when children get out of cars and walk through the yard to get a close-up view of the puffed-up crowd of cartoon characters and holiday heroes. They also have toys and treats waiting in a sleigh to give to children who come by in December.

When it comes to inflatables, people either love them or hate them. The Richies unabashedly love them!

You won't see many inflatables at the home of Marvin Perkins in Magoffin County, but his Christmas display may cause you to pull over on the Mountain Parkway. It is not the biggest holiday display in the state, but it may be one of the most prominent. It is a landmark for travelers, and the first thing they see when they cross into the county if they're going south on the parkway is a blast of light on a dark stretch of road.

In this roadside attraction, lights hang from the eaves of the farmhouse and barns and drape the trees. Over the years, Perkins had made many animated figures, such as deer that jump the fence or Santa waving from a helicopter.

Perkins said he is happy to light up his corner of the county as a tribute to Jesus, the "light of the world."

One warm Christmas tradition takes place in a cold, dark place. Since 1975, people have been going underground for the annual **Mammoth Cave Sing**. Normally, group sizes are limited in the world's longest cave, and reservations are recommended, but on the first Sunday of every December, it is a free-for-all party atmosphere. As many as seven hundred people show up to sing carols in a large room not far from the cave's entrance.

Park rangers said this organized event is just the latest example of music being bounced off the cave walls. Park ranger Dave Spence said there are early visitor accounts of people singing in the cave and playing musical instruments. He suspects Native Americans also sang in the cave, and there are records of regimental bands playing there during the Civil War.

History shows that in 1883, some local folks dragged a decorated tree into the cave and sang carols. Spence said that the tree stayed in place for decades until it caught fire, probably from a torch carried by visitors.

Different performers lead the singing each year. In 2022, it was the Lindsay Wilson College Singers. "The acoustics are amazing in there. We love it," said Dr. Gerald Chafin, the college's choir director. "We like to think we are singing 'rock-a-pella' music for everyone!"

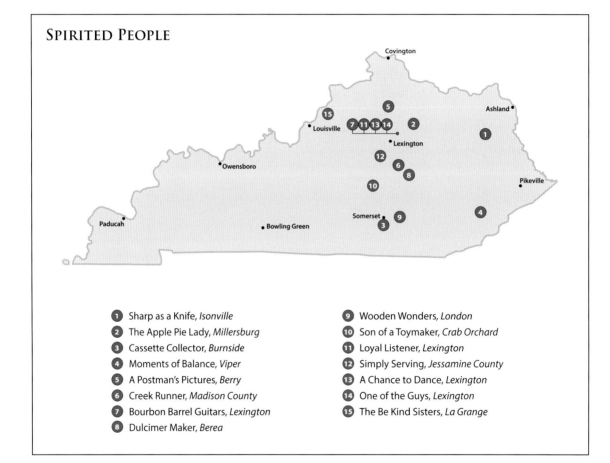

SPIRITED PEOPLE

1. Sharp as a Knife, *Isonville*
2. The Apple Pie Lady, *Millersburg*
3. Cassette Collector, *Burnside*
4. Moments of Balance, *Viper*
5. A Postman's Pictures, *Berry*
6. Creek Runner, *Madison County*
7. Bourbon Barrel Guitars, *Lexington*
8. Dulcimer Maker, *Berea*
9. Wooden Wonders, *London*
10. Son of a Toymaker, *Crab Orchard*
11. Loyal Listener, *Lexington*
12. Simply Serving, *Jessamine County*
13. A Chance to Dance, *Lexington*
14. One of the Guys, *Lexington*
15. The Be Kind Sisters, *La Grange*

SPIRITED PEOPLE

SHARP AS A KNIFE

ISONVILLE

Art collectors from all over the world have been to a small shed that sits next to a one-story house in rural Elliott County. It is the workshop where Minnie Adkins has carved out a name for herself.

"I hear I'm recognized nationally and internationally as a folk artist," she said. She is not sure how that happened but can confirm she has had visitors from a lot of places, including Switzerland.

She really noticed an uptick in interest in her work after she was featured in the 1989 book *O Appalachia: Artists of the Southern Mountains* by Millard and Ramona Lampell and David Larkin.

Minnie Adkins, a well-known folk artist, carves many whimsical creatures in her living room in Elliott County.

When she is not in the workshop, you can usually find Minnie in her living room with a towel in her lap, whittling away at a piece of wood. "Oh, I love it," she said. "I don't like to be called a folk artist. I like to be called a wood carver."

The chips fall where they may as she expertly shaves the bark off sticks with a sharp blade. "You ain't never supposed to whittle toward yourself, but I do sometimes," she said.

It is something she has done since she was a little girl, carving things to play with because her family couldn't afford toys. She made yo-yos, slingshots, pop guns, and wooden animals.

In 1968, Minnie and her husband, Garland, moved to Dayton, Ohio, in search of factory jobs. She continued to whittle. He helped, cutting out the shapes that she refined and painted. She gave most of her carvings away but sold a few at flea markets. She got homesick, and they moved back to Kentucky in 1983.

In 1986, when she was fifty-one years old, Minnie noticed a carved goat at an art gallery in Morehead and told the owner she had similar pieces at home. He told her to bring them in, and he would try to sell them. She still has the bill of sale, showing she made $32 for four carved figures. That is how she was "discovered." Now collectors will pay hundreds of dollars for just one of her carved animals.

"In the beginning, it was all about the money, you know, and paying your electric bills and all that," Minnie said. "I've learned a yard sale is good, a flea market is better, a gallery is better than that, and a museum is where it's at!"

Garland died in 1997, and she vowed to never make another carving. It was something they did as a team. But after a while, she picked up her pocket knife again, realizing whittling gave her comfort as well as a steady income. She married Herman Peters, a pipe fitter, in 1999, and he, too, got the bug to be artistic. He worked with metal and made several giant iron roosters along with some other animals modeled after her carvings before his death in 2008.

Minnie has received many honors, including the Distinguished Artist Award from the Folk Art Society of America in 1993 and the Appalachian Treasure Award from Morehead State University in 1994. In 1998, she and

Garland (posthumously) received doctor of humanities degrees from Morehead State, with the university recognizing the value of art learned through a nonacademic process.

Her pieces are in a lot of museums, from the Kentucky Folk Art Center in Morehead to the Smithsonian Institution in Washington, D.C. They are also in private collections of celebrities such as Oprah Winfrey and Barbra Streisand. More than 170 of her carved creations sit on a table in the Lexington home of Mike Norris, the retired director of communications for Centre College. He has written four children's books, illustrated by pictures of Minnie's carvings. He sends her ten rhymes at a time, and within days, she has figures to match them. Their most recent collaboration is *Ring around the Moon*, a collection of what Norris calls "Mommy Goose" rhymes.

Her carvings are of things such as bright blue roosters, smirking skunks, and sheep singing from songbooks. She also carves figures from the Bible, such as Noah and Adam and Eve. Others are purely from her imagination. As she held up a creature with a purple face, green ears, and a pink-spotted belly, she said, "I don't know what it is or who I'm making it for, so I'm going to call it a Who-What!"

"Art is not about clutching something and holding it tightly but sharing it with other people, and when you're free enough to do that, you'll be rewarded," Norris said. "I've seen that over and over again with Minnie."

Now, in her ninth decade, Minnie is still as sharp as her knife and has no intention of slowing down.

"I hope and pray God will keep me able and keep my eyesight until He gets ready to take me home," she said.

The third Saturday of each July is "Minnie Adkins Day" in Elliott County. It is marked with an arts and crafts market in Sandy Hook that draws collectors and vendors from several states.

THE APPLE PIE LADY

MILLERSBURG

Busy travelers may speed right through the small Bourbon County town of Millersburg as they drive on U.S. Route 68, but for people in the know, a certain banner is like a stop sign. It displays the mathematical symbol for pi (π), and if you stop, you might just meet the Pie Lady.

Mary Lou Rankin makes fried apple pies in her small kitchen behind the building that used to house her family's hardware store, which was in operation from 1968 until 1996. She ran Rankin Hardware most days while her late husband, Robert, worked as a plumbing contractor. She never

Mary Lou Rankin has made handmade apple pies in her small kitchen for more than forty years.

thought about selling her pies until the Millersburg Volunteer Fire Department burned down in 1975. Many women in the community organized a series of bake sales to help the department rebuild. People have been asking for her pies ever since.

"They do want my recipe," she said with a twinkle in her eye. "But I don't give out my recipe. If they want to pay for it, then that's another thing!" She didn't say how much she would charge for it.

Her pies are made to be handheld, filled with dried apples and a secret mixture of spices.

Mary Lou can barely turn around as she makes the turnovers, but a little corner of her kitchen is all she needs to make her magic. Flour covers the countertop as cooking oil sizzles in the electric skillet. She places the pies in one at a time and knows just when they are brown enough to remove from the oil to be placed on paper towels to cool.

Her son, Gaylen "Frosty" Rankin, is an accomplished painter with an art studio in the old store, but he knows when people come up to the window, they are often looking at his mother's handmade sign advertising pies.

"I would say the business here is 80 percent pies, 20 percent art," he laughed. "Mom adds a secret ingredient—love. And you can't get that at McDonald's."

For several years, Mary Lou also set up a concession wagon at summer and fall festivals in the area. She said she often sold four hundred pies or more in one day at those events. She also held bake sales in the hardware store before Easter and Mother's Day where jam cakes and cream candy were just as popular as the apple pies. People in Bourbon County anticipated those sales and poured in to grab up the goods as soon as she unlocked the door.

Mary Lou has been referred to as the "Matriarch of Millersburg." There aren't many projects in the town of eight hundred people that haven't seen her thumbprint. She has led beautification efforts, planting flowers in the town square and worked with the Fireman's Auxiliary to raise money for a playground. In the winter, she also caned chairs for customers, a skill she taught herself.

Customers who spend some time with Mary Lou are also likely to hear her take on politics. She prefers Democrats but encourages everyone to vote no matter which party they like. She also has a lot to say about the weather, cooking, the old hardware store, her sons, her pets, and the people she has met.

So how famous are the pies? She has made them for former Kentucky governor Steve Beshear and award-winning jockey Pat Day and once sold fifty-three pies to a busload of daytrippers from Jessamine County.

"I got on the bus and felt like a celebrity," she said. "They were taking my picture and shaking my hand and getting autographs."

I met Mary Lou when she was eighty-seven, and she said she had no intention of putting up the skillet. "I've worn out a lot of them," she said.

"I enjoy all of it," she said. "It's keeping me busy and on my feet. If not, I would probably just sit down in a chair, and first thing you'd know, I'd be in a nursing home." She tells everyone who will listen that hard work is the key to a sharp mind. She kept that work ethic even after two bouts with cancer.

People who visited Mary Lou's kitchen in the years after the hardware store closed found the pies were $3 each. The conversation was priceless.

CASSETTE COLLECTOR

BURNSIDE

When John Platt goes to his garage, it is not to get a tool or check on his car. He is opening the door to his man cave, which is also like a museum of music from the 1970s through the 1990s. The garage is filled with audio-cassette tapes, which most music companies stopped producing more than twenty years ago. Shelves line all four walls, from floor to ceiling, filled with tens of thousands of cassettes.

"I get them from all over the world," he said.

"I enjoy it because they're durable and easy to have around, and a lot of music that has been transferred to digital has been lost through the years. I have tapes I can't even find on the internet," Platt said.

Platt has been trying since 2016 to get into the *Guinness Book of World Records*, but there is no recognized category for audiocassette tape collections. Still, the chronicler of such records has corresponded with him about what it would take to be listed in the book. He has been told that no duplicates can be counted for the world record and that no homemade mix tapes will be allowed. Each cassette must have a barcode and must play from start to finish.

Platt assembled a panel of adjudicators in 2018 to verify the size of his collection, but it was a tiring, multi-day task to record the titles of each cassette and test that each one worked. The panel included local radio disc jockeys and an owner of a record store.

"The first time we tried to do an official count, it took four hours just to get through the A's," Platt said. All the cassettes are shelved alphabetically.

John Platt's happy place is his garage filled with cassette tapes.

Platt said Guinness was not satisfied with his documentation at that time. He has tried a couple of times since to send pictures and videotapes of his collection to add to the logs previously submitted.

"They keep asking for more paperwork," he said. "I won't give up because I want to put the record in my son's name, and it would mean a lot to him."

Platt said his son, John Platt Jr., has autism and didn't speak until he was seven years old. "Listening to music in the garage is what got him to say his first words," Platt explained. He also said his son helped him find a lot of the cassette tapes by going with him to yard sales and flea markets.

The largest collection Platt has discovered in his research is about ten thousand tapes, which he can beat easily. He had 18,315 when I visited him in January 2017. Six years later, the number had grown to more than 35,700 and was still growing.

"I've never seen one I didn't want," Platt said.

Although most people think of cassettes as being fragile, that doesn't concern Platt. He can get them working again quickly by using pieces of tape to splice breaks. If the plastic cartridge is beginning to separate, he uses a cigarette lighter to melt it back together.

Platt likes all types of music, from Merle Haggard to Fleetwood Mac, Alice Cooper to Ella Fitzgerald. But he has a clear favorite.

"If you don't have Pink Floyd in your collection, you don't have a collection," he said.

Vinyl records have made a comeback. Could the same thing happen with cassettes?

"I have not lost hope," Platt said. "Since I started this, it has surprised me to find out how many people still love them."

He said 75 percent of his collection has been given to him, and he gets new ones in the mail almost every day. He has built an addition to his garage once and is willing to do it again if he needs more room for shelves.

"I just love everything about cassettes," he said. "They sound better to me. They're my passion, and I will keep collecting them whether I get in the record books or not."

MOMENTS OF BALANCE

VIPER

There is something about Adam Fields and streams. At least once a week, you can find this Perry County man wading in a creek, searching for rocks, just like a kid.

Fields looks for rocks with interesting shapes, divots, and varying weights—solid rocks he will turn into fragile pieces of art.

"I went through a divorce when I was in my early thirties, and I was devastated," Fields said. "I was just so anxious. I didn't know what to do with myself. Then I remembered rock balancing, and I started doing it just to find something soothing to relax my mind."

Fields became fascinated with rock balancing in 2014 when he saw a man doing it on a YouTube video.

"It was amazing. It saved me," he said. "It was a godsend."

Rock balancing takes an incredible amount of patience, something Fields has in abundance. The meditative pastime involves turning a rock by fractions at a time until it catches in a crack or divot on the rock beneath it. Once that rock is standing on end, Fields adds another, then another, until he has a precarious tower of rocks that is always on the verge of toppling.

Fields has made hundreds of these temporary towers, and, in his hands, the seemingly impossible task looks easy. He tries to snap a picture of each creation if he can get his mobile phone out quickly enough. He shares the photos on his Facebook page (*Kentucky Rock Balancing Art*).

"People have a hard time believing it's possible," he said. They think that he uses glue or wires or that the images are Photoshopped. "Some of my friends joke with me that it has to be some kind of black magic or voodoo."

The moment of balance can come in an instant. Fields may tinker with a group of rocks for an hour before everything comes together. "You can

A balanced rock creation by Adam Fields stands just long enough to be photographed.
ADAM FIELDS

feel the vibration going from the bottom to the top. It connects. It's like magic when gravity lines it up," he said. "It never gets old."

Fields is not just an artist who wanders along riverbanks. He is a licensed chiropractor who also balances spines. He jokes that he wants his patients to say, "My doctor rocks!"

The art of rock balancing is not the same as rock stacking, which is discouraged in national parks and forests. Hikers often leave flat rocks stacked on top of each other on trails or in creeks as landmarks or memorials, inspiring other hikers who come along to build their own stacks. These mounds of stone multiply and can stand for months. Conservationists say

Adam Fields searches a stream for one more rock as he attempts to go higher with a balanced tower. HAYLEY ADAMS

they can cause erosion, affect animal ecosystems, and destroy the natural beauty of a site.

Fields understands those concerns and subscribes to the "leave no trace" practices of true nature lovers. He balances rocks only in creeks near his home, and the rocks are returned to the water before he leaves a site.

Even though the works of art take an hour or more to construct, they often disappear in seconds after Fields declares them complete. Just a breath of air can knock them over, and that's okay with him. It is reminiscent of the way Buddhist monks destroy a sand mandala after laboring over it for hours, symbolizing that life is always in flux.

"You have to learn to let things go," Fields said, "even things you work hard to achieve."

A POSTMAN'S PICTURES

BERRY

When Mark Bradford leaves the tiny Berry post office each morning, he knows he is in for a day filled with give-and-take. He will give out letters and packages and take a lot of pictures.

"You never know what you're going to see," he said.

Bradford has been delivering mail for more than two decades, most of those years on the back roads of his native Harrison County. His daily route is ninety-two miles long, with 515 mailboxes.

A few years ago, Bradford began to lose enthusiasm for his job. He was going through a divorce and feeling depressed. You might say he was

Mark Bradford documents life in rural Harrison County by taking photographs with his mobile phone as he delivers mail.

A friendly dog knows Mark Bradford carries treats along with the mail.

MARK BRADFORD

mailing it in. Then he recalled how much he enjoyed photography classes when he majored in art at Eastern Kentucky University. He addressed his boredom by snapping pictures with his iPhone, documenting things he saw on the mail route.

Now he treats his route as a daily treasure hunt for interesting pictures.

"I take pictures of everyday occurrences, and everybody could do that if they'd just stop and say, 'That's a great picture,'" Bradford said.

Bradford said even though he takes the same route every day, he sees it differently at various times of the year. He knows the roads and homes so well that he notices even slight changes, such as when a tree falls, a fence gets painted, or a cow has a calf.

A few years ago, he started posting his pics on his Instagram account (@pappybradford). "God blesses me with all this beauty, so I take pictures, and I want to show everybody," he said. Those posts led to something he never dreamed would happen.

Directors at the nonprofit Boyd's Station Project for photojournalism students started following his account and found that his pictures fit their mission of documenting rural life in Harrison County. Soon, founder Jack Gruber, who is a photographer for *USA Today*, had Bradford signed, sealed, and delivered as an exhibitor at Boyd's Station Art Gallery in Cynthiana.

"I've got Charlie Brown luck, so I didn't tell anybody because I didn't know if it was going to happen or if they'd pull the football away from me," Bradford laughed.

It happened. For several weeks in 2022, visitors came to the gallery to see an exhibit titled *Rural Route Collection*. The curators had a major job sorting through Bradford's bundles of images. At the time, he had about six thousand pictures stored in his phone. "Fortunately, we have a lot of photographers and editors," said Maggie Heltzel, Boyd Station's artistic programs director. "It was a blast for them to pick which photos to use and to curate a show like this."

Heltzel said she believes the people who saw the collection loved the familiarity of it. Many people who came to the exhibit's opening night live on Bradford's mail route. No doubt, some of them hoped to see an image of their home, farm, or neighborhood.

Bradford has come to realize he is packaging a record of life in the country. He will stop to take pictures of a turtle in the road or reflections in a puddle. Many of his pictures are whimsical, such as a dog standing on a backyard trampoline or a goat climbing on a dry-docked boat. When it comes to framing and composition, he will go the extra mile, often returning to his route after work to "chase sunsets."

"I've taken pictures of barns that aren't there anymore," he said. "They've fallen down. It's documenting my route and the changes of life, really."

Bradford's first-class look at life is a lesson for all of us to stop and smell the roses or at least take a picture of them. Even familiar journeys can lead to surprise destinations. After his exhibit closed in Cynthiana, some of his photographs were shipped to New York City to be featured in a gallery there.

He hopes his work delivers the same message to everyone who sees it: "Enjoy the world around you. That's what I'm doing."

CREEK RUNNER

MADISON COUNTY

Curtis Eades spends long days working in hot, dirty conditions, picking up piles of trash. He does it by choice and without pay, loving a job most of us would hate. And when he comes home, he often unwinds by making art.

"There's so much I want to paint and do and not enough time to do it," Eades said.

He puts brushes to bottles he has collected and literally turns trash into treasures.

"It's definitely cheaper than having to go to a craft store and buy all the materials," he said. He gets his art supplies by the bagful from creek banks and ravines.

Curtis Eades started his mission of collecting trash by cleaning up a section of Tates Creek near his home.

As he paints in the loft of his home in rural Madison County, he can look out a window and see Tates Creek and hear the calming sound of rushing water. But in 2019, Tates Creek was a sorry sight.

"I looked out over the water one day after it had been raining, and the creek was way up," Eades said. "And I just watched five mattresses float by. Immediately, there was anger, there was frustration, and, before you know it, I was running up and down the creek cleaning up whole sections."

That is how he got his nickname "Creek Runner." Now his almost daily trash collecting trips have become an exercise regimen for him. Friends helped him pick up fifteen thousand pounds of trash in 2021. They truly find joy when they are down in the dumps.

"Because if you do it, you might as well make it fun, right?" said Eades. He posts videos of his creek running on social media, hoping to demonstrate to others that it can be rewarding to clean up the world around you. He has received feedback from people all over the globe who say they have been inspired to do the same thing in their communities.

"I've heard from people from coast to coast, Maryland to California, and gotten messages from Nigeria and people in India," he said. "It's a great feeling." They follow his efforts on Facebook at *Creek Runner 242*.

One of the people he has inspired is Whitney Lewis. The Jessamine County woman is an avid hiker and kayaker. She decided on Earth Day 2023 (which was also her birthday) to start collecting bags of trash each time she was in the woods or on a waterway. She set a goal of collecting five thousand bags of trash by the end of the year but ended up doubling that. Governor Andy Beshear named her the Beautify the Bluegrass award winner for 2023.

For Eades, trash collecting has become a passion and a full-time job. He said he mostly "works for nature" these days, but he makes a little money to support his mission by selling his artwork on Etsy. Fans can pick up painted bottles or sculptures made of jugs and jars, wires and tires. He said he often envisions what he will create when he picks up certain pieces of trash. What he does is called upcycling, a way to reuse items that would otherwise end up right back in landfills.

Every day is like a treasure hunt. "You name it, I've found it," he said.

He does caution others who want to do what he does to wear gloves and boots. He sometimes comes across dangerous items, such as discarded syringes, and has encountered snakes and poison ivy.

After Eades cleaned a ten-mile section of Tates Creek near his home, he moved on to Owsley Fork Reservoir south of Berea, a beautiful place for boating and fishing. But that beauty was marred by illegal dumps found in many of the ravines that feed water into the reservoir.

"Water is life, and these creeks and streams are the veins of the planet," Eades said. "We're clogging them up with our trash."

The dirty work would seem overwhelming to most people, but Eades can see a brighter day. He often speaks to school groups and believes younger generations "get it" and will be better stewards of the land and water.

"Yeah, the trash is horrible," he said. "But I get to be out in nature all day. There's nothing horrible about that."

BOURBON BARREL GUITARS

LEXINGTON

Mike Mankel has been playing music for more than fifty years. He hopes it is as smooth as his favorite Kentucky product.

"I moved here in 1991 and became a fan of bourbon and bourbon culture," he said.

The Pennsylvania native, who came to Kentucky to work in medical sales, has always dabbled in woodworking. He said one day in 2012, the idea just came to him to try to make a guitar from reclaimed wood, probably while he was enjoying a sip of whisky. He sees gracefulness in the shape of a guitar and beauty in barrels, so why not combine the two? He did

Mike Mankel's guitars retain all the markings of the bourbon barrels he uses to make them.

some online research and could find only a couple of luthiers who had ever turned barrels into stringed instruments, and one of them was in Ireland. It appeared to be an untapped market.

It didn't take him long to turn his idea into reality. Mankel taught himself how to take three barrel heads and a couple of staves and turn them into playable works of art. He wants his electric guitars to look as if they came right out of the rickhouse—that they aged right along with the barrels that housed bourbon for twenty years.

Mankel said he has enough discarded barrel heads to build guitars for the next decade, but he is always looking for more. He gets them from distilleries all over central Kentucky, such as Woodford Reserve or Buffalo Trace. He wants to keep the stamps and stains intact and likes the appearance of a white oak barrel that has been charred by fire on the inside. The charring is what gives bourbon its color and brings out the flavors of the sugars in the wood.

He cuts staves into small pieces and fits them into a frame to make the curves of his guitar bodies. "Basically, it's like a child's puzzle. You pick what fits and discard what doesn't," he said.

Mankel has produced nearly fifty guitars at his Bourbon Barrel Guitar Company in Lexington, which is a one-man operation. "The old saying is, 'If it was easy, a ton of people would be doing it,'" he said.

It takes about 150 hours to make just one guitar. Prices start at about $7,500. Mankel knows it takes a special buyer to take one home.

"It's very rewarding, but, oh my gosh, it's a lot of effort," he said. "I want them to sound excellent and cost so much I couldn't afford one!"

The instruments are never far from their roots. Just like the original barrels, each guitar holds some of the product. There is a compartment for hiding a flask built into the back of each one, and Mankel pours a little bourbon into that space so the guitars can maintain the intoxicating aroma of his favorite beverage.

"It goes in, and you swish it around, and now the guitar is happy," he laughed, saying he thinks of the guitars as living beings.

Many of the aged and amplified guitars have been purchased by people who don't play music. They display them as pieces of art, which is just fine with Mankel.

"I just feel positive pride that my hands, my work, my instruments are appreciated."

The guitars are something to see, each with unique markings and perfect imperfections, but it is also fun to hear them—barrels of fun!

DULCIMER MAKER

BEREA

Warren A. May has pep in his step when he goes to the workshop behind his home each morning. There are so many projects to finish, so many orders to fill. People all over the world know him as a master maker of mountain dulcimers.

"They could be cut in some modern ways, but people know I cut them by hand," May said while turning a knothole into the image of a humming-bird at his workbench. "Each one is a little different."

Warren A. May has been making dulcimers since 1972.

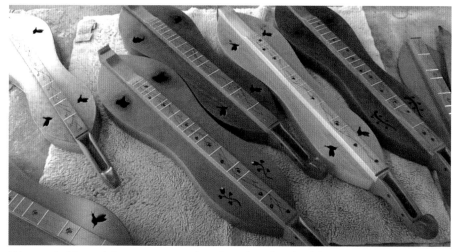

Warren A. May's dulcimers are works of art, handcrafted from native woods.

May fell in love with the traditional Appalachian instruments while teaching industrial arts in Louisa, Kentucky, in the 1970s. He said he was inspired by other musicians in the schools and the community. "I made one and then immediately started making ten. Then the word got out."

In 1977, May left teaching and moved with his wife to a farm in Berea, where they raised three daughters while he developed a reputation for woodworking. He sold dulcimers and wooden furniture from a shop in the city's well-known crafts district. The quality of his handiwork struck a chord with musicians and art collectors. He said he was amazed how quickly news spread of his love for making dulcimers, especially when he was just starting out.

He said his big break came after he had been in business for five years. The Smithsonian Institution ordered one hundred dulcimers and sold them through its gift catalog. May filled that order in ninety days and that set a production pace he has kept ever since.

The catalog exposed May's work to an international audience. Now all it takes is a quick search on the internet to find him. When I visited his workshop, he had just finished packing up a dulcimer to send to a customer in Singapore.

May said when the uninitiated are introduced to the mountain instrument, they are hooked because it is so easy to play. "Three strings and two notes, and you can sing almost any ballad or country or gospel song," he said.

Historians say the simple instrument first appeared in the mountains of Appalachia in the early nineteenth century and may have roots in Scotland or Ireland. May notes that dulcimers are mentioned in the Bible (Daniel 3:15). It is in the zither family of stringed instruments. May believes dulcimers were popular among mountain people during the Great Depression because they were easier and cheaper to make than a violin. The instrument gained notoriety outside of Appalachia in the 1960s, when Jean Ritchie, a Kentucky folk singer, played one in performances in New York City.

May numbers each dulcimer he creates, and by the end of 2023, he hit number 19,300. That means he has averaged more than one a day over the past half century. It is unlikely any other person has made as many dulcimers as May or ever will.

"Not from scratch," he said. "Some of the music shops in Arkansas have made many, many more, but they have streamlined the process with much less handwork."

It is that handwork that makes his dulcimers pieces of art, crafted from native woods as varied as cherry, walnut, and tulip poplar. Prices start at $400 and go up to $1,200, depending on the wood and the level of decoration.

May worked out of a retail shop in Berea for forty-two years but closed it in 2019, and he is selling now through a website and Facebook (*Warren A. May Dulcimer Shop*). He said he is "semi-retired," but it is difficult to tell. He still goes to his workshop every day to carve wood, sing, and enjoy life. As I pulled away on the day of my visit, with car windows down, I could hear him strumming a dulcimer and singing the old gospel tune "I'll Fly Away."

WOODEN WONDERS

LONDON

Jim Sams spends several hours each day in his home art studio, but he doesn't feel cooped up. He is surrounded by images of nature—delicate flowers and colorful songbirds he created, inspired by his lifelong love of the great outdoors.

"I spend a lot of time in the woods," he said. "I'm not a hunter, but I love to hike, and I soak in the sights around me. I remember my dad taking me on a trail and showing me wildflowers, and that stuck with me. I still enjoy seeing them in the spring."

A hummingbird carved by Jim Sams appears suspended in flight as it drinks from a wooden wildflower.

Sams said he always wanted to be an artist. As he was growing up in eastern Kentucky, he was exposed to the unique craftsmanship of black-smiths, basket makers and weavers, quilt makers, and furniture artisans. He said, "Their dedication to their craft was instilled in me at an early age." He has adopted their meticulous approach to creating art.

Sams is a self-taught artist. In the mid-1970s, he started working with wood, first making duck decoys. He said some of the first ones were rough looking. But after he got good at making ducks, he wanted to do something more challenging, turning to the things he would see on his hikes.

Now his creations are a multistep process. He starts by cutting out the shapes of birds, leaves, flowers, or butterflies on a band saw. One piece may contain several types of wood. "I use a lot of buckeye and basswood and tupelo gum for the flowers. I may use hickory for the stems," he said.

He then carves features by hand, doing a lot of sanding, and uses a wood burner for the fine details, such as the lines in a feather. The painting takes the longest time, and Sams said it is the hardest part of the process, but it is what brings the creations to life. He doesn't cut corners, taking pride in being precise.

Sams purposely adds imperfections to his wooden leaves and petals, just as you would see them in nature. A laurel leaf may have a hole in it or be brown around the edges; an azalea may appear to be wilting or have a bug perched on a petal. When he displays his work at art shows, people often think Sams is selling wooden vases, not realizing the flowers aren't real.

"They have to touch them," he said. "They don't believe they're wood." Sams chuckles to himself every time a potential customer bends over to try to smell one of his flowers. That's the ultimate compliment.

In 1979, Sams quit his job as a bookkeeper to become a full-time wood artist, a decision he has never regretted. "I feel guilty sometimes because I know people struggle with work and are not really happy about it. I love what I do and know I am very blessed."

As his work became more complicated, Sams carved out a name for him-self as someone who could freeze in time the fleeting beauty of a flower in bloom or a bird in flight. His wooden hummingbirds are his most sought-after item. They seem suspended in midair, drinking nectar from flowers.

Sams has traveled a lot to show and sell his work, most often at the Southern Highlands Craft Fair in Asheville, North Carolina, where he has been an exhibitor for more than thirty years. In 2020, he was one of 120 people invited to display their work at the Smithsonian Craft and Design Show in Washington, D.C. That ranked him as one of the best of the best.

His carvings range in price from $500 to about $3,000 and can be viewed on his Facebook page (*Jim Sams Woodart*). "It's an honor that someone would want to have my work in their home," he said.

Retirement is not in his plans. His work may be delicate, tedious, and time consuming, but for Sams, there is no better way to whittle away the hours. "I'm very content to sit at my worktable and carve."

SON OF A TOYMAKER

CRAB ORCHARD

A visit to Chuck Knerr's office is like going to a toy museum. Shelves and cabinets are filled with some of the most successful toys of the twentieth century—things such as the Hula Hoop, Frisbee, Water Wiggle, Silly String, and Super Ball.

Rich Knerr (Chuck's father) and Spud Melin were the inventors of those toys and hundreds of others through their company Wham-O. The high school friends started making toys in a garage in South Pasadena, California, in 1948. Now, more than seven decades later, Chuck is producing a toy in a garage in rural Kentucky.

Chuck Knerr produces the Whirly-Go-Round in his Kentucky workshop, after thinking about it for more than sixty years.

It is a toy kids can spin on, using only their core muscles to control it. Chuck calls it the Whirly-Go-Round. His dad tried to make something similar in 1961. Chuck declares it "the best toy Wham-O never made."

"The prototype Dad made was an accident waiting to happen," Chuck said. "It was metal, and your legs got tangled up. He was constantly warning me to watch out because it wasn't a finished product. They just let it go, but I never let it go. I just kept thinking about it."

The original spinning toy idea never got off the ground because, at the time, the company was swamped with filling orders for one of its most successful toys, Slip 'N Slide.

As a child, Chuck was a test pilot for almost everything his dad made. "Testing the toys was a joy," he said. "There were a whole lot of toys, and not all of them were good," Chuck said. For example, Wham-O marketed a mink stole for navels, "for the person who has everything, even a belly button!" It was a flop.

Despite testing hundreds of toys, the one that never got made was Chuck's favorite. "We were in the space race with the Russians, and I felt like an astronaut spinning on that thing," he said.

His version, the Whirly-Go-Round, is built to last. It weighs thirty-five pounds and is made of bamboo and steel bearings. It sells for about $300, which, Chuck knows, makes it a high-end toy. He wants it to be an heirloom that gets passed down from generation to generation.

Chuck calls his creation an "indoor thrill ride" and said parents have told him they love it because it gives their children some "old-fashioned fun and exercise." It gives them time away from electronic screens. He said children like to make themselves dizzy and cites research from Penn State University that indicates spinning can help a child develop depth perception, improve their concentration, and gain a good sense of body awareness.

Rich Knerr died in 2008 but not before encouraging his son to give toy making a spin. Chuck feels as if his life has come full circle now that he has picked up where his father left off.

"As I'm working alone putting these together, I often think about my dad and know how much he would enjoy this if he could be here participating in some way," Chuck said.

Chuck named his one-man, one-toy company "Spud 'N Rich" to honor the creators of Wham-O. They sold the company in 1982, and various companies have produced Wham-O products since then.

Chuck retired from a career in marketing and moved with his wife to a farm in Kentucky in 2021 because they wanted to get away from big cities. They chose to settle outside Crab Orchard after being struck by the region's beauty while driving through the state. Chuck said as soon as they found the right property for sale, they packed up and became residents of the Bluegrass State. The farm he lives on has given him the peaceful life he said he needed to focus on his lifelong dream of producing the Whirly-Go-Round.

In this day of electronic toys and tablets, Chuck doesn't know if kids will be immediately enamored by a spinning toy as he was six decades ago, but after they try it, he is confident they'll come around (and around and around).

LOYAL LISTENER

LEXINGTON

Kroger shoppers in downtown Lexington know the face of John Short. He has been bagging groceries for more than twenty years, first at the Romany Road store and now at the location on Euclid Avenue near the University of Kentucky campus. If he speaks to customers, there is a good chance they will know his voice as well.

It is a voice that has been heard on Lexington sports talk radio shows for the past four decades.

When Short is not at work, he is likely parked in front of a radio and parked on hold, waiting to talk to the host of a sports show about his

John Short is glued to the radio each morning, waiting for his chance to call in to multiple sports talk shows.

Ryan Lemond, cohost of Kentucky Sports Radio, expects to get a daily call from John Short.

beloved Kentucky Wildcats. "They're good to watch, good to follow, and I'm happy to have followed them for a good long time," said Short.

Ryan Lemond, cohost of Kentucky Sports Radio, which is heard on stations across the state, expects to get a call from Short every time he is behind the microphone, and he knows how the conversation will go.

"First, he's going to call me 'a great American,' then he's going to give me a prediction, and he's always going to say Kentucky will win," Lemond said.

Short's first call to a radio show was in 1985 to talk to legendary UK play-by-play announcer Cawood Ledford. "I just remember on that first call I said they were going to win, and that's about it," he said. But he loved it that he was able to talk one-on-one with someone he had listened to for years.

That started his call-in passion. He has been predicting the Wildcats will win in every phone call to a radio host since then, no matter the sport, no matter the opponent. He calls points "bigguns," as in "Kentucky is going to win by twenty bigguns."

Listeners have come to love Short's positivity and his homespun phrases. Instead of answering "yes" to questions, he says "okey-dokey" or "yes indeedy."

Two days before I interviewed Short at his home, he had called in to *Big Blue Insider* on WLAP-AM and assured the host the UK men's basketball team would beat the University of Evansville "by thirty-five bigguns." That night, Kentucky lost by three points.

When Short called again the next day, host Dick Gabriel asked him if he had learned a lesson. "I believe I did," Short said.

"And what was that lesson, John?"

"Never overlook anybody," he replied.

Gabriel said people he meets in public often ask him about Short, and few seem to tire of hearing him call in even though his conversations seldom vary.

"People genuinely like John," Gabriel said. "He's built a fan base of his own."

During another call that same week to KSR, Lemond teased Short about his large-margin prediction. "John, that's a very liberal score you picked. You're a very liberal guy," Lemond joked.

Short, somewhat defiantly, shot back, "I'm not liberal. You know that." When the morning sports shows end, Short stays tuned in to conservative radio talk shows and sometimes calls in to them as well.

Tom Leach, the current play-by-play "Voice of the Wildcats," said there is a curiosity among listeners who may tune in to hear if there is ever a situation when Short would make a prediction against UK, whether it be basketball, football, volleyball, or baseball. "I don't think we will ever see it," Leach said.

The frequent caller has lost 90 percent of his vision due to glaucoma. He said that is part of the reason he loves radio so much—the announcers help his mind see what his eyes cannot. And that mind is always working. One of Short's talents is the ability to tell people he meets what day of the week they were born on. If he is given a date, he can quickly calculate where it fell on the calendar.

Calling the shows is just part of Short's daily routine, and he admits he sometimes falls asleep waiting for his turn to talk.

"When I'm put on hold for an hour, I just lie on the bed, and I do snore sometimes," he said. Lemond and the other hosts on KSR, Matt Jones and

Drew Franklin, sometimes crank up the volume so listeners can hear Short snoring. It is all in good fun.

"John Short is my favorite caller of all time," Lemond said. "He is in the Sports Radio Hall of Fame because you know he's always going to bring a smile to your face."

He's not really in a hall of fame (not yet), but Short is famous with listeners, and when it comes to UK fans, he's a biggun, yes indeedy.

SIMPLY SERVING

JESSAMINE COUNTY

Kids and kitchens are not always a good combination. It is so easy to make a mess or to get in the cook's way. But Bailey Sissom loves it when her kitchen is full of children. Several times a month, she conducts baking classes for young people, showing them how to make the kind of treats they really enjoy, such as customized cupcakes and holiday-themed cookies.

The former elementary school teacher said she really got focused on cooking in 2013, when she became a stay-at-home mom. She taught herself how to prepare easy meals that could feed her family for a week.

Many of the teens and preteens come to her classes week after week because of the welcoming environment.

"The classes are really fun because we can learn new cooking techniques," said twelve-year-old Hadley McMillen. "And she always gives us a recipe to take home so we can practice and work on those skills."

But there is a sweeter purpose to the classes than just making tasty desserts. They help fund Sissom's nonprofit organization called Simply Serving.

Sissom had a large commercial kitchen installed in a building in her backyard in 2019, soon after she survived a scare. Earlier that year, she left an oncology appointment with the belief she had lymphoma and would be starting chemotherapy. For five days, she stressed about how she would care for her husband and three young boys. Then she got a phone call saying it was a misdiagnosis.

"I still don't know what happened or why, but it gave me the opportunity to have a really unique perspective of what it's like to at least start down that journey," she said. "I love to cook, so I just decided I am so grateful, I'm going to pay this forward." Her relief turned to action.

Volunteers prepare easy-to-fix meals to be delivered to families dealing with cancer.
BAILEY SISSOM

She went on Facebook and asked friends if they knew of a family that was dealing with cancer and could benefit from a freezer full of healthy meals. "I immediately got eighteen responses," she said. That was the start of Simply Serving.

Now she and a team of volunteers meet twice a month to prepare meals for families with a member undergoing cancer treatments. The families are nominated, their friends make online donations, and then a portable freezer is filled with a month's worth of easy-to-fix meals. They prepare things such as pulled pork barbecue, stuffed peppers, breakfast burritos, and chicken meatballs.

Sissom said it is better than a meal train where friends sign up to supply dinner on different nights. This way, the food comes all at once. She said there is not as much waste because families can use it over time when they need it the most. But she knows most families don't have the storage space for twenty-five to thirty frozen meals. That is why Simply Serving always supplies a small freezer and picks it up when the food is gone.

Since its beginning, more than three hundred volunteers have helped prepare meals, and Simply Serving's "fleet" has grown to twelve freezers that are always in circulation.

When ten-year-old Macie Monroe of Lawrenceburg was diagnosed with non-Hodgkin's lymphoma, Simply Serving posted her story online and got a meal package fully funded in less than two hours. Sissom said that was a record.

"It doesn't surprise me," said Macie's mother, Kellie. "When we found out Macie had cancer, we opened our door the day before chemo started, and we had a community of people on our front lawn praying. The support has been amazing."

"Insurance does pay for everything we're going through medically, but when you're having to rip and run down the roads and having to worry about eating out and things, the costs add up," said Macie's father, Jason. "Simply Serving was just a blessing."

The family was able to quickly put meals on the table during the several weeks Macie was going through chemotherapy. They were fueled by the food, and Macie was fueled by documenting her journey online.

"I wanted to share my story for kids who also get cancer, so they can search my YouTube channel (*Macie Lynn*) and know how it feels," Macie said. She ends most videos with these words of encouragement: "Remember, you guys are stronger than you think!"

Simply Serving has a simple purpose—to take one worry off the plates of families going through a tough time. It is a recipe with several steps, starting with kids who make cupcakes and ending with a freezer full of blessings.

"I get so much from doing this as well," Sissom said. "It's awesome to see the families so appreciative."

A statement on the nonprofit's website sums it up best: "We can't offer a cure, but we can eliminate stress."

Due to the rising cost of groceries and supplies and a dwindling number of volunteers, Simply Serving changed the way it operates in 2024. Instead of meeting biweekly, the organization now focuses on an annual meal prep event that lasts for a week. Bailey Sissom's S.S. Cooking School still offers regular classes to support the mission of providing meals to cancer patients and their families.

A CHANCE TO DANCE

LEXINGTON

Jenna Lyon does not want her Sunday dance class at a Lexington studio to be different from any other class she teaches, but it is. It is made up of students who may not be expected to succeed, who are often defined by what they cannot do. But through dance, Lyon helps them find what they can do, and it is quite a lot.

Longtime members of A Chance to Dance are Anna Juett, Madeline Mandina, Will Robeson, Olivia Ash, and Mallory Burrows. JENNA WARD

"I don't make their class any easier," she said. "I don't try to change things because I don't think they're capable of doing something. They're really capable of doing anything. It just takes more time, more breaking things down, but they're truly amazing, and I love working with them."

Lyon, who started taking dance lessons at age three, launched her A Chance to Dance program in 2013, when she was still a student at Scott County High School. She was inspired to take on the challenge after seeing a group of students with functional needs dance at a performance in Louisville. At first, she had four students with Down syndrome, autism, and other physical or learning obstacles. By the time she was a senior at the University of Kentucky in 2017, she had twenty dancers in her troupe and a team of volunteer helpers.

None of the dancers pays for lessons "because a lot of their parents have extra expenses for medical bills and therapies and different things," Lyon said. "I didn't want the cost to keep anyone from participating."

Sara Robeson of Georgetown said the classes help her son, Will, develop social skills. "He never misses a class, and he talks about it all week," she said. "It is his favorite activity."

You hear the same thing from parent after parent.

Karen Juett said when her daughter, Anna, first started coming to the classes, she would sit at the edge of the room and just watch the other students. "But now she gets up there and has big movements. We're really proud of how much her confidence has grown," Juett said.

Student Lucy Harding said she can't imagine her life without the classes. "Having a place where I can come and just be myself and be who I am without being put down or criticized for what I do wrong feels amazing," she said.

The real test of confidence for any dance student is a recital. Lyon works for months to get the students ready to perform for a crowd made up of family members, friends, and supporters. Excitement is in the air each spring as they wait backstage for their moment to shine. The girls get into sequined costumes, and the boys put on tuxedo jackets and bow ties. For years, Lyon has teamed up with Lexington's Barbara Ann's School of Dance for a recital in the auditorium at Transylvania University.

When the A Chance to Dance group takes the stage, the routine is important, of course, but people pay more attention to the smiles than the steps. Once-shy children now soak up the attention and applause.

"I would like to know what the world would be like if we all had the same outlook on life and love for life that my students do," said Lyon, who is affectionately referred to as "Miss Jenna" by the young dancers.

So what can students with learning and physical challenges do? For one thing, they can use their footwork to bring a crowd to its feet. The group never fails to receive a standing ovation after performing for an audience.

⌇

A Chance to Dance now has its own studio in Georgetown, and there is a waiting list to get into classes, which take place several times a week. Jenna Ward (marriage changed her last name) tries to pair each dancer with an assistant and has at least thirty volunteers willing to help, including her husband, brother, and sister. Her mother is on the nonprofit's board of directors, and her father provides "financial and moral support."

ONE OF THE GUYS

LEXINGTON

In January 2019, two best friends spent several hours a week working on their dance moves as they prepared for a big performance coming up later that spring. They were learning to clog to "Uptown Funk" by Bruno Mars.

Brack Duncan was the teacher. He has been a competitive clogger since he was in elementary school. When he was in high school in Clark County, Duncan began working with adults with functional needs, helping them develop social skills. He took a special interest in Josh Banks of Winchester.

"I think there is a reason for every characteristic and ability you have," Duncan said. "It is just finding out how to use it."

Duncan thought Banks would find his abilities if he were around people more often, so he started taking Banks to hang out with his FarmHouse fraternity brothers at the University of Kentucky. It became their Friday thing—playing pool, watching television, and going out to lunch. Those were ice-breaking moments for both the college students and thirty-three-year-old Banks.

Duncan said it wasn't long before everyone was taking Banks under their wings.

One of Banks's favorite things to do is ride in trucks and sing country songs along with the radio. That also became a big part of their Fridays, with Duncan behind the wheel as the pair rode around campus or Lexington neighborhoods. Banks drummed on the dashboard as Duncan cranked up the volume on his favorite songs.

"We're not even talking so much in those moments but just being and existing, letting him do his thing, and letting the joy he gets out of that spread onto me and pour out onto others," Duncan said.

Josh Banks became a full-fledged member of the FarmHouse fraternity at the University of Kentucky through his friendship with Brack Duncan. SOPHIE DUNCAN

In the fall of 2018, the fraternity's president, Ben Bohannon, got the idea to make Banks a member. He discussed the idea with the other brothers, and they approved it by a unanimous vote. That made Banks the first person with Down syndrome to ever be inducted into a social organization at the university. As far as Duncan can determine, Banks was the only such member at any university in the nation.

As Banks sat in a leather chair during a ceremony in his honor, tears streamed down his face as his emotions overwhelmed him. Then he wiped his cheeks and joined his new brothers in a boisterous fraternity chant. Banks, a man of few words, simply said afterward that he was happy. "I like hanging out with my friends," he said.

I asked," Is everyone here your friend?"

"Yep."

Banks was inducted as an "associate member" only because he was not a student. But Bohannon said Banks has the same rights and privileges as any other member. When that year's composite photo came out, Banks was pictured along with everyone else.

"You look for honesty, integrity, spirituality," the president said. "Josh wholeheartedly wants to make those around him better. That's what pushed him over the edge for us and let us know he belonged here."

The emotional induction ceremony is something each brother will remember.

"It really is a big step in history," Duncan said, "not only for the special needs community but for all of society and the world to see this inclusion and witness love in its purest form."

After Banks and Duncan got their dance moves down, they taught the routine to the other FarmHouse members to perform at the spring Greek talent show on campus. It was a showstopper, with Banks getting the loudest ovation when he stepped into the spotlight.

Banks said he wasn't nervous at all, just happy.

He's just one of the guys—a fraternity man who never took classes but gets straight A's in friendship.

THE BE KIND SISTERS

LA GRANGE

La Grange has dubbed itself "the kindness capital of Kentucky." From the time you cross the city's borders, the telltale signs are everywhere—on patios, in yards, and in store windows. The force behind the movement is two small girls with a large collection of spray paint.

In 2019, Raegan and Rylyn Richins had an idea that caught on like wildfire. Raegan was ten years old; Rylyn was seven.

The girls said they were on a long road trip and tired when the family car had a flat tire. "I guess we were mad at each other," Rylyn said, recalling how grumpy everyone was because of the delay in getting home. Once they were back on the road, she said they saw a simple handmade sign in a yard that read, "Be Kind."

"That made us happier," Raegan said. "And we said we should do that in our yard. Because it brought us a little joy, we were like, 'Hey, we can do the same where we live.'"

Four years later, Raegan and Rylyn couldn't go anywhere in Oldham County without being recognized as the "Be Kind Sisters." They are the county's goodwill ambassadors.

"At first, we just started making signs, and we were thinking it would be a test run," Raegan said. "We took them to some places, and people really liked them and wanted more."

The sisters also wanted to promote compassion because of their love for children with learning and physical challenges. Their parents, Ryan and Rhonda Richins, adopted two children with Down syndrome after their brother, Kallen, who also had the disorder, died shortly after birth. Their older sister, Kendall, who also had Down syndrome, died in 2021 at age sixteen.

Rylyn and Raegan Richins have made thousands of "Be Kind" signs, which are seen in yards and windows around the world. RHONDA RICHINS

"We noticed some people weren't being kind to them," Raegan said. She said they thought maybe the signs would be a reminder to others to consider their words and actions when dealing with people with disabilities.

Their parents said the girls came up with the idea to make signs on their own. "They truly did it because they wanted to be the voice of kindness for their siblings, for our family, for this community," said their mother.

The girls had set a goal of making sixty-five signs, but by the summer of 2023, they had made more than five thousand. Their backyard is a sign-making assembly line, with a picnic table filled with spray paint cans, wooden block letters, and stencils. The signs also come with designs, such as a dog paw, peace signs, hearts, unicorns, or the American Sign Language symbol for love.

Their signs have shown up in yards coast to coast. When the girls were interviewed live from their home by Hoda Kotb and Jenna Bush Hager on NBC's *Today* show, they were surprised when the control room switched to a shot of a massive electronic billboard over New York's Times Square sharing their "Be Kind" message. Rylyn said that was "mind-blowing!"

Their mother said, "We also have friends that took some signs to China. That was huge!"

The owner of Mainly Creative, a La Grange gift shop, said Be Kind signs are one of her biggest sellers. Sometimes, the sisters will bring her twenty signs in the morning, and all will be sold by afternoon.

The signs sell for $10, and all the proceeds go to charities the girls support, such as food banks, animal shelters, and organizations that help people with Down syndrome. They have raised more than $50,000.

La Grange is known as Kentucky's Kindness Capital because Raegan and Rylyn lobbied the mayor and city council to make the designation official.

"The vote was eight to nothing," said Mayor John Black. "Well, probably nine to nothing since I got to vote myself along with the eight council members. It passed with no discussion. It went down quickly. It was one of those no-brainers."

The movement has paid off in waves. The girls and their hometown have been featured in national news articles and television segments. HGTV produced an episode of *Home Town Kickstart* in La Grange and had artists paint murals throughout the city, giving it a happier look to match its reputation. Each mural illustrates the kindness theme.

Rhonda said she doesn't believe one sign can make a difference for everybody, "but it has made a difference for them and their friends."

"I had a friend tell me she was just not having a great day, and then she saw someone wearing a Be Kind shirt," Rhonda said. "Immediately, she thought of the signs and the girls, and it changed her attitude."

But the girls want people to do more than plant a sign in their yard. Rylyn said people "should just add small, teeny acts of kindness into their day, maybe like smiling at someone who is lonely or just holding the door."

Rhonda said she and her husband, Ryan, who is a police officer, have wondered if their daughters are ready to retire from the project, which has become a major consumer of their time.

"Their dad asked if this is something they still want to do, and they were staunch in saying, 'Yes, absolutely.'"

They don't sell their signs online or outside of their home area. That is just too much to take on. So the girls encourage others to make their own signs. They often meet with church, school, and scout groups to share their mission.

"It's perfect that other people are making Be Kind signs," said Raegan. "That means kindness is spreading."

MORE PEOPLE TO KNOW

There are many other people who have been featured in *Spirit of the Bluegrass* segments who deserve mention for their love for the state and special ways of spreading joy:

- Shaun Washington may be the best-known tour guide in central Kentucky. His banter with guests and knowledge of the horse industry makes his Unique Horse Farm Tours by bus an unforgettable

Shaun Washington takes tourists inside the barns at some of Lexington's most beautiful horse farms. UNIQUE HORSE FARM TOURS

experience. He has hundreds of five-star reviews on Trip Advisor and entertains customers with stories of driving celebrities to elegant Kentucky Derby eve parties. Among those he has chauffeured are Zsa Zsa Gabor, Priscilla Presley, Muhammad Ali, and Danny Glover.

- Benjamin Williams of Bardstown displays entrepreneurial spirit. At age fourteen, he convinced a bank to loan him $10,000 to buy an old box truck and, with his father's help, converted it into an ice cream truck. His mother steered the truck to events because Ben wasn't old enough to drive. There is always a long line when Ben's Jammin' Ice Cream truck shows up outside a school or at a festival.

- Another young Kentuckian getting noticed is Phoebe White of London, who taught herself to yodel at the age of seven by watching old cowboy movies featuring Roy Rogers and Gene Autry. Her jaw-dropping skills helped her win several singing competitions and led her to produce an album that landed on the western charts. At age thirteen, she performed on the stage of the Grand Ole Opry in Nashville, singing along with one of the best-known cowboy bands, the Grammy-winning Riders in the Sky.

- Lucas Etter of Lexington became a celebrity among puzzle enthusiasts in 2016, when, at the age of fourteen, he broke the world record for solving a three-by-three Rubik's Cube. He solved the puzzle in 4.9 seconds, making him the first human to break the five-second barrier in a competition.

- When he was eight years old, Jonathan Rader of Nicholasville attended a show featuring an Elvis Presley tribute artist. He nudged his dad and said, "That's what I want to be when I grow up." But he didn't wait. Soon after that, he was performing as "Little E," winning competitions and getting Elvis fans all shook up. He now often finds himself onstage with some of the nation's top Elvis impersonators.

- People with unique hobbies or collections are always great subjects for a television report. When Don Saager of Stamping Ground retired as a tool and die maker in the late 1990s, he took his love of trains to a whole new level. He decided to build a full-blown steam engine from scraps of metal he had around his workshop or found in junkyards. It was big enough to sit on and powerful enough to pull passengers, so, of course, he needed a track to run it on. He started with a small loop of track. That turned into a railroad that now covers five acres, goes a mile into the woods, and has a tunnel and a trestle. Many hobbyists who have miniature trains have small tracks in their backyards, so it is a treat for them to bring their engines to Saager's "Heavenly Hilltop Railroad" to run them on a much longer line and take in the scenery. It is quite a sight to see grown men and women gleefully playing with trains and lining up to ride them. Saager prefers live steam, but his track also welcomes diesel engines and electric ones.

- Even though Brian Gorrell is retired, he spends a lot of time working in the basement of his Lexington home and even more time playing. He plays discs produced in the days before radio on machines that allowed people to enjoy music in their home. Gorrell has collected more than two hundred phonographs, including some of the earliest ones produced by Thomas Edison's company in the 1880s that play wax cylinders. The retired band director also repairs phonographs and sells them. He finds the buyers are mostly young people who are fascinated by something that works so well and sounds so good without electricity.

- One of the world's top chainsaw artists lives in Webster, Kentucky. Abby Peterson said he was at a low point in his life and without career goals a few years ago when he prayed for guidance while cutting timber. "There was a stump there, and a voice in my head said, 'Carve a bear head.' So I carved a bear head." And the rest is history. A man offered Peterson $200 for that carving, so he decided to make some more and soon got really good at it. Now chainsaw carving is Peterson's full-time job. He carves images of all types of animals as well as Native Americans, cowboys, Bigfoot, and bugs. He also helped make the world's largest Smokey Bear, which is on display in South Dakota. In 2022, he won the top prize at the Chetwynd International Chainsaw Carving Competition in British Columbia.

- A Scott County doctor is in a race against time to save a historic structure on a piece of property he bought in 2012. The crumbling stone building was a dormitory for Choctaw Academy, a boarding school for Native Americans that operated from 1825 to 1843. Dr. William "Chip" Richardson, a Georgetown ophthalmologist, bought the farm solely because he didn't want to see the remnants of the school fall away to nothing. "There's such a grand story of empowerment in this place," Richardson said. His research revealed more than six hundred boys from seventeen tribes were educated at Choctaw Academy, and some of them went on to attend Transylvania University and become doctors, lawyers, and teachers. Richardson is seeking grants and donations to restore the roof and shore up the walls. He envisions a day when school groups and history lovers can come get a feel for what it was like to be a student at the school nearly two hundred years ago.

- There may be nothing tastier than a home-grown tomato. Bill Best of Berea knows that better than anyone. This former literature teacher and swim coach is an expert on seed saving even though he never took a class in agriculture. It is a skill he has preserved from his childhood. Best has grown more than five hundred varieties of heirloom tomatoes and more than a thousand types of beans over the past forty years and has written two books on seed saving. He saves the seeds of everything he grows and loves showing people how easy it is to separate the seeds and dry them. He has a freezer full of seeds that will still be good for starting gardens fifty years from now. His table is always the most popular one at farmers' markets in Lexington and Berea. Buyers often say they will never eat a grocery store tomato again after tasting the redder, juicier, more interesting ones Best lays before them.

- Authors are often worthy of recognition. Sean McHugh, a caricature artist at Walt Disney World, maintains a love for his hometown of Maysville. The picturesque city on the banks of the Ohio River is home to an old hospital, theaters, and historic homes that are said to be haunted. It is where McHugh developed a love for all things Halloween related and used his cartooning talent to write and illustrate the *Broomsticks* series of children's books about a friendly young witch and warlock. His niece, Katie McHugh Parker, is his coauthor.

McHugh calls his works "love letters to Maysville," and visitors to the city will recognize many of the places pictured in the books.

- When Charles Bishop of Mount Sterling moved into a house that was built in 1795, he had no idea it came with a dark story. It is on land that once housed a fort known as Morgan's Station. Bishop began to research the fort's history and found it was once well known as the site of the "last Indian raid in Kentucky," an incident from 1793 that had been largely forgotten. He used his research to write a novel titled *Morgan's Station*, a work of fiction based in fact about the attack that led to two deaths and the capture of nineteen settlers. Bishop said he was careful to be sympathetic to both the pioneers and the Native Americans who were trying to cohabitate in the wilderness. A lot of authors travel the world for inspiration. Bishop is proof that sometimes all you have to do is walk out the front door.

UNEXPECTED SPIRIT

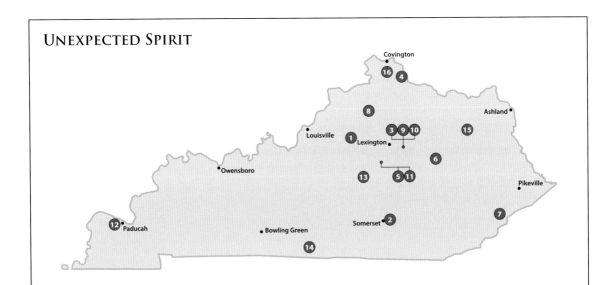

1. Lincoln Look-Alikes, *Frankfort*
2. Crazy Car, *Somerset*
3. Geek Church, *Lexington*
4. Punkyville, *Falmouth*
5. KCAL Old-Time Radio Theater, *Nicholasville*
6. General Store of the Airwaves, *Stanton*
7. Calls from Home, *Whitesburg*
8. Larkspur Press, *Monterey*

9. Thoroughbreds for Sale, *Lexington*
10. Racetrack Superstitions, *Lexington*
11. Primate Rescue Center, *Jessamine County*
12. Dippin' Dots, *Paducah*
13. Dead Fred, *Danville*
14. The Marble Club Super Dome, *Tompkinsville*
15. Home for Wayward Babydolls, *Elliottville*
16. Disco Bathrooms, *Florence*

UNEXPECTED SPIRIT

LINCOLN LOOK-ALIKES

FRANKFORT

The sixteenth president of the United States is revered in the state of his birth. If you want to emulate someone who is looked up to, six-foot-four Abraham Lincoln is a monumental choice.

The Association of Lincoln Presenters has 150 members throughout North America, and each year they gather in a place that played a significant role in Lincoln's life. Many times, the group has conferenced in Kentucky.

Lincoln was born in a log cabin near Hodgenville in 1809. His family moved to the nearby Knob Creek Farm, where the future president lived from age two to almost eight. The family left Kentucky in late 1816, moving to Spencer County, Indiana, but Lincoln kept ties to the Bluegrass State throughout his life. In 1842, he married Mary Todd, the daughter of a wealthy Lexington attorney.

In 2017, nearly a third of the Lincoln presenters met in Lexington, each one of them the rail-splitting image of the Great Emancipator. The look-alikes made day trips to Frankfort to see the state capitol and Kentucky History Museum and to Nicholasville to visit the Camp Nelson Civil War Heritage Park. The Mary Todd Lincoln House in Lexington was also a stop on their itinerary.

Stanley Wernz of Cincinnati has averaged more than one hundred appearances per year portraying Lincoln. He said, "It's a joy to see the places he visited and try to experience the things he experienced."

It can be comical to see so many Abe-L bodied people get off a bus and walk single file through city streets, donning stovepipe hats. Many of the pretenders are accompanied by spouses who try to mimic Mary Todd

Abraham Lincoln presenters gather around a statue of the boy who would become president in Hodgenville in 2017. RON CARLEY

Twenty-eight Abraham Lincoln presenters pose for a photo at the Lincoln car deal-ership in Frankfort in 2017. MARY ARMSTRONG

Lincoln. One Jefferson Davis look-alike even snuck into the 2017 confer-ence. Everyone was civil.

"Lincoln said, 'Let's not be enemies but friends,'" said the Davis pre-senter, David Walker of Van Wert, Ohio. "He said we both read the same Bible and pray to the same God, so why should there be malice toward me?"

The group members are traffic stoppers. When you look like a shiny penny, honestly, there is no hiding. Many people jumped out of their cars or came out of their businesses to take selfies with the Lincolns as they walked the sidewalks of Frankfort. There was a gaggle of photographers waiting at the state capitol to take pictures as the presenters circled the Lincoln statue that stands in the rotunda.

"Next to Jesus Christ, he is probably the most recognizable man on Earth," said Ron Carley, a presenter from Detroit.

During these conferences, almost every moment is spent thinkin' like Lincoln. Some of the men have been doing this for scores of years. Others are new at it, but they all got into it because of their looks.

Carley said he showed a $5 bill to his barber and asked him to cut his hair like Lincoln's. He was amazed by the result. "Other than being six-four, I never thought I looked like Lincoln before that."

That was the beginning of a beloved pastime for Carley, who now goes dressed as the former president to every festival, parade, and school gathering he can.

Jim Sayre, a longtime presenter from Lawrenceburg, Kentucky, said, "I've seen a lot of people who could portray Lincoln. You won't get rich at it, but you won't go broke, either." He recalls making enough prize money in a look-alike contest during one of his first outings as Lincoln to cover the $50 cost of his rented costume. That was in 1983.

Some of the presenters speak at schools, churches, or living history events. They are expected to be experts on Lincoln's life. Others are mostly posers.

James Mitchell of Hope, Kansas, goes to a lot of political rallies just for the fun of it. "I just go and do it. I don't usually get invitations. I just show up," he laughed.

The Mary Lincolns do not want to take a back seat at the conferences, taking advantage of the available educational opportunities. They say she was much maligned, and they want to set the record straight.

Susan V. Miller of Jessamine County said, "She kept him [Lincoln] abreast of current events. She helped him with his manners. They were a true partnership. I don't think he would have been president if not for Mrs. Lincoln."

The group is looking for younger men to wear the beard. Many of the presenters are in their senior years, outliving Lincoln, who died at age fifty-six.

"I'd love to do it another thirty-four years, but time takes its toll," said Sayre.

One thing is certain: Abe Lincoln is still popular whether he is living in the present or reliving the past.

CRAZY CAR

SOMERSET

The roads around Pulaski County are always busy. Traffic isn't something you pay much attention to—unless one particular car comes into view.

Bill Grider's 1995 gray Toyota Tercel is like a rolling toy museum or art exhibit, covered with trinkets and treasures from the tip to the top to the trunk. He has no idea how many things he has glued to his car. One person who tried to count them figured it was about eighteen hundred.

"It's like trying to count chickens," Grider said. "You can't count 'em. They just dart around all the time."

The crazy car was born in 2015, when Grider fastened a plastic parrot on the front because he always liked hood ornaments. He just thought it would

Bill Grider's 1995 Toyota Tercel was a rolling art exhibit around Somerset from 2015 to 2023.

look good. At first, the parrot had a battery-controlled sensor that detected the presence of passersby. It would squawk, "Polly wants a cracker," surprising anyone who got close. That feature stopped working after a few weeks.

Grider liked the reactions he got so much that he decided to glue a few more things to the hood, mostly Happy Meal toys from McDonald's or figurines of familiar playthings, such as Barbie dolls, Power Rangers, or Teenage Mutant Ninja Turtles. Two years later, it became difficult to find that first decoration among the crowd of creatures, cartoon characters, and key chains glued to the car's body. Almost all of them were given to him by children.

"They've given me rocks, and they've given me sticks," he said. And he was happy to glue them alongside the other decorations. He uses automotive Goop glue, which he said is superstrong. He never worries about anything blowing off.

Grider knows many of the items are collectible, and he has been offered a lot of money for some of the pieces, but he said not one of them is for sale. He pointed out a plastic yellow horse on the roof. "Two truck drivers offered me $100 for that horse, but I wouldn't take it on account of the kids. They like seeing it."

Most people of any age can't help smiling when they see the artsy auto.

"Man, this is truly amazing," said Doc Kanarowski, who saw the car for the first time in the parking lot of a restaurant. "It would bring happiness to anybody."

Well, anybody but one recent bystander.

"She cussed at me and said, 'How do you see to drive that crazy-looking trap?'" Grider told her, "Lady, I can't see, but I live around here, and I pretty much know where I'm going!"

When I rode with Grider, he was eighty-eight and getting along just fine. He loved showing me around Somerset and delighted in the honks and waves he got from other drivers as they passed him on the road.

He said as long as he keeps his line of sight clear in the windshield and mirrors, he doesn't expect to get in any trouble with police. I can confirm as a passenger that, despite all the things glued to the hood, it was easy to see the road in front of him. He glued the taller items to the roof or side doors.

Decorating the car became a hobby for Grider after the death of his wife, Jewell. He said his adult children are somewhat embarrassed by his car,

The view from the front seat of Bill Grider's car includes the backsides of dozens of plastic figurines.

but that doesn't bother him. He believes parents are supposed to embarrass their children.

A local newspaper published a story about Grider's car and quoted him as saying he hoped it would help him attract a woman. He regretted that the statement made it into print. He told me it was a joke, and he feared it misrepresented his motive, which he insisted was just to bring a little glee into the lives of children who saw him driving around.

He does have another car that he takes on long trips, but he doesn't like it as much. He would rather drive the Tercel that is bedecked with seashells, clowns, bobbleheads, and dinosaurs.

Every time Grider hits the road, it is a joyride. The car is the talk of the town, and he believes there is still room for more conversation pieces.

"Yeah," he said. "I could put a hundred more on there."

※

Just before Bill Grider died in 2023 at age ninety, he put the car up for sale with a Somerset used auto dealer. But it didn't sit on the lot long. After a couple of weeks, he went back and took it off the market. He missed it too much. I believe that if he had had a say in the matter, he would have asked that the hearse that took his body to the cemetery be decorated with a few whimsical embellishments.

GEEK CHURCH

LEXINGTON

The Lexington Comic and Toy Convention has been going strong since 2011, becoming one of the largest such gatherings in the Midwest. Nearly thirty thousand people attend the four-day event each spring to celebrate superheroes, fantasy art, robots, and aliens.

Author Lydia Sherrer of Louisville knows it as a magical way to meet her fans. Several of her young adult novels about wizards and witches flew off her vendor's table at the 2018 convention.

Dave Mattingly conducts a Geek Church service at the Lexington Comic and Toy Convention in 2018.

The Comic-Con attendees go to search for books, costumes, posters, and figurines. But before they poured onto the floor on Sunday morning, a few of them also did some soul-searching.

Sherrer was one of about a dozen people who found their way to a room in the Hyatt Regency Hotel next to Lexington's convention center, which was set up for a service called Geek Church.

Organizer Dave Mattingly told the congregation, "I like to reach out because you are my people. I am a nerd in almost all ways."

The Louisville man has been conducting church services at Comic-Cons around the region for more than fifteen years. He has literally worked as a rocket scientist, an engineer, a computer programmer, and an improvisational actor. He said he was an atheist until a business partner helped him see the Bible in a new light. Now he is a born-again Christian.

"My friend was a real Christian living it out," Mattingly said. "I saw the joy, hope, and love and all the ways he was serving people and started to feel that tug at my heart."

Mattingly is not a licensed minister, just what he calls a "rogue operative for the Lord." He is involved in several Christian geeky groups, such as Costumers for Christ and Grave Robbers, which is a Bible study group for "goths and punks."

Mattingly, a frequent vendor at Comic-Cons, said he hated it that Christian exhibitors often didn't have time to worship on Sundays when attending out-of-town events. "I started this just so we would know we are not alone. I'm not the only Christian who likes board games and weird movies. We're everywhere."

His nondenominational church services are somewhat traditional. There are praise songs and the sharing of communion, but the sermon topics are unique.

Mattingly said, "I've preached about aliens and *The Walking Dead*, whatever, to find a spark to reach the audience I want to reach."

At the Lexington event, he talked about the infinity stones that are key to the Marvel Universe movies, drawing parallels to how Christians can combine their skills to make a difference. "We are different infinity stones," he told the congregants, some of whom were seated in cosplay costumes, dressed as characters from the *Harry Potter* books. "As we spread the gospel, we become more powerful, and the gates of hell shall not prevail against us."

Mattingly said the casual approach is what works for him. He conducted the service wearing a well-worn T-shirt from the Christian Gamers Guild. Text on the shirt paraphrased Proverbs 16:33, reading, "We may throw the dice, but the Lord determines where they fall."

Sherrer loves that she doesn't have to give up going to church when she is at a convention, and she believes God smiles on these unique gatherings. "He takes incredible joy in all these amazing things that geeks are doing," she said. "All these creative imaginative things reflect what He created us to be!"

After the final "Amen," the congregation went back to the exhibit hall, hunting for classic toys, comic books, or customers. Mattingly hoped some of them had already found what they were looking for.

PUNKYVILLE

FALMOUTH

There is a growing town along U.S. Route 27 that you won't find on a map, established in 2003. It is about two miles south of Falmouth.

The self-proclaimed mayor and his wife are the only residents, and he named the town for himself: Punkyville.

"I've had that nickname since I was a pup," said Charles "Punky" Beckett. "They always called me that. A lot of people don't even know my real name."

Beckett, an army veteran who spent most of his life working for a paving company, built his tiny town for a simple reason: He needed a place to put

Charles Beckett's storage buildings resemble a small town known as "Punkyville."

his stuff. He collects antiques and novelty items, old cars, and conversation pieces. But he didn't want to store his collections in boring warehouses. He decided to build storage sheds that look more like a movie set. The fronts of the buildings, lined up in a row, resemble a general store, a dentist's office, a gas station, a hotel, a post office, and a church, among other things. Items on display inside each building match the theme.

He has a favorite thing to collect. "Signs. Any kind of metal signs," he said. "You can't get enough signs." He does have a lot of them, from gas stations, barbershops, and other long-gone businesses.

Inside the buildings, you will see such things as a pump organ, manual typewriters, a mail truck, leather postcards, and vintage vending machines. A B&O Railroad caboose holds things train buffs love to see, such as lanterns, crossing signs, and passenger schedules.

Visitors drop by Punkyville almost every day. It has become an unintentional string of museums, not really meant to be a tourist attraction. There are no business hours. Beckett welcomes lookers any time and wouldn't dream of charging admission. "Most of the time, I walk around with them," he said. "But if someone comes and I have to go somewhere, I say, 'You all just look around. I'm gone. I've got stuff to do.'"

Beckett said there is no way to put a value on what he has accumulated, but he salvaged a lot of it or got it for a bargain. "They always said when I was young, I was cheap," he said. "When I would go out with girls, I would buy one Coke and get two straws."

He has been offered a lot of money for some of the items. He said one metal sign is worth $1,400, but nothing is for sale. He collected the items because he likes them, not because he is trying to make a profit.

As the complex grew, the sheds developed the look of a western town, especially after Beckett added a replica of a jail. He said children love to go in there and pretend they are cowboys or bank robbers. He hopes his Main Street is a place where imaginations run wild.

Punkyville is experiencing growing pains. Items hang from the rafters in one of his largest storage buildings, and it might be time to expand. Beckett said he believes he may build two or three more buildings. "Then, after that, there will probably be another one," he said while laughing.

Many people come to Punkyville for photo shoots, and there have been nearly a dozen weddings in the chapel. The mayor gets immense joy out of sharing his creation. You may have to go out of your way to visit Punkyville, but visitors say it is a detour worth taking.

Punky Beckett died on February 1, 2021, at age seventy-five. His wife, Joyce, and their four children plan to keep his village intact and open to the public. "He wouldn't want us to dissolve it," Joyce said. "He worked too hard on it."

KCAL OLD-TIME RADIO THEATER

NICHOLASVILLE

There is no other theater group in Kentucky quite like the one that performs in the back room of a former store on Nicholasville's Main Street. This troupe puts a new twist on some old material—radio comedy and drama scripts from the 1940s.

Five times a year, the players for KCAL Old-Time Radio Theater perform for an audience. Four of the shows are in the theater. The other is a dinner show at a winery. The shows are also recorded as podcasts and archived on the group's website. Listeners who tune in without knowing about the theater group might think they have gone back in time. There is a real KCAL television station in Los Angeles, but these adopted call letters stand for "Creative Arts League," the umbrella organization that helped fund and promote the arts in Jessamine County when the radio theater idea was hatched in 2014.

Director Doug Fain said there are two reasons the group formed: "One, we wanted to give back to the community, and, two, we're all pretty much hams."

There are a dozen regular cast members, and many are familiar faces in Jessamine County. Fain is the circuit clerk and the morning air personality of the local FM radio station. Coproducers Norman and Denise Cline have performed in local theater over the years. David Damron is a banker, Billy Holland is a minister, and Connie McDonald is a retired teacher. But faces don't matter in this so-called theater of the mind.

Members of KCAL Old-Time Radio Theater promote an episode of *Gunsmoke*. Pictured, from left: Doug Fain, David Damron, Cooper Bartlett, Denise Cline, Norman Cline, Galisa Watts, Billy Holland, Connie McDonald, and Eddie Clements. In front: Susan Clements and Steve Watts. KCAL OLD-TIME RADIO

Actor Carolyn Threlkeld jokes, "I can play a tall thin blond on the radio, and nobody ever knows that I am not!" She is also often assigned child roles because of her ability to mimic little girls and boys.

If they are done well, you should be able to enjoy these shows with your eyes closed. But if you're in the audience with your eyes wide open, you are also in on some secrets. You can watch the actors take turns making sound effects, which can be as simple as pouring water into a cup or knocking on a wall. Shaking a sheet of metal sounds like thunder; scrunching bags of cornstarch sounds like a person walking in snow.

"This is a place I can come and be as silly as I want to be, and it's accepted and sometimes applauded," said Norman Cline.

Each of the KCAL players has been on a stage before performing in traditional plays, but there are differences when you do a radio drama. Denise Cline said the biggest contrast is obvious, and it is a huge one. They don't have to memorize lines. Each actor has a script in front of them. "That's the best," she said.

That doesn't mean theatergoers just watch people standing around reading. By the time the shows are ready for an audience, they are well rehearsed and polished into something visual with mood lighting, stage movement, and costumes. An "On-Air" light indicates when the recording has begun, and a flashing "Applause" sign prompts audience reaction.

When the shows were first performed in the golden age of radio, there often was a live studio audience, especially for comedies. The laughter and applause were genuine. Fain said, "We try to make it look like it would've looked back then, but I'm sure if some of the actors from the 1940s were to see us, they would roll a couple of times in their grave!"

Copyright laws have changed over the years, and Fain has found plenty of scripts from seventy or eighty years ago that are now available for free download. The group has performed episodes from such comedies as *Fibber McGee and Molly* and *Father Knows Best* and dramas such as *Dragnet* and *Gunsmoke*.

A typical performance opens with a crooner singing a hit song from the 1940s and includes commercials from that time for products that were heavily advertised, such as Ovaltine, Reynolds Wrap aluminum foil, or Roma wine. When an announcer talks about the benefits of smoking, it brings chuckles from the audience and is a reminder of how things have changed. Two half-hour programs are re-created. To add to the small-town charm of the experience, audience members gather in the lobby during the intermission to be served free homemade baked goods.

The KCAL crew must be doing something right. Just like in the 1930s and 1940s, the audiences gather around the radio even though it is a prop on center stage. When a show ends, many of the regular patrons immediately reserve seats for the next show even though it will be three months away. There are usually three performances of a show, but an extra matinee is often added to meet demand. The theater can seat only fifty people, so shows sell out quickly.

KCAL members say the shows wouldn't work as well in a larger space. "I like that you can look right to the back row and make eye contact with the people sitting there," said Norman Cline.

In addition to providing entertainment, Fain said the group wants to give back to the community. It organizes a gospel concert each year featuring local talent to raise money for the Jessamine County Schools Homeless Education Fund.

In these days of streaming video on demand, Spotify, and TikTok, KCAL Old-Time Radio is a blast from the past, a look at how the masses used to get their news and entertainment.

"I don't know how long it will last," Fain said, "but as long as we're able to keep selling tickets, we will keep performing."

GENERAL STORE
OF THE AIRWAVES

STANTON

One of the complaints about radio stations these days is that they have lost their identities. Listeners note that the hosts are often national personalities and that the playlists are preprogrammed. But there are still some hometown stations that thrive because they stay local and resist change.

People who drive around Stanton every day around 10 a.m. are likely tuned to the same radio station where they hear the familiar greeting, "Good morning, eastern and central Kentucky, and welcome to *Tradio*!"

For more than forty years, WSKV-FM has been the home of *Tradio*, an on-air swap shop. Such programs are popular on many radio stations throughout the state's mountain region, with names such as *Swap Shop*, *Trade Mart*, and *Trading Post*.

Tammie Watson is a longtime listener to *Tradio* and sometimes seller. She said it is not to be missed. It is about more than buying, selling, and trading. It is pure entertainment and a way to get to know your neighbors. Callers often talk about their health or the weather, and they announce things such as school plays and church revivals. "It's a show that's very much community oriented, and you never know what you're going to hear," Watson said.

On a typical show on a Thursday morning in March, callers offered up everything from kayaks to kittens to tires to railroad ties.

Angela Oldfield, the station's program director, said *Tradio* is her favorite show to host. "It seems and feels social," she said. "I feel like I'm hanging out and talking on the phone with my whole family."

Angela Oldfield is one of the regular hosts of *Tradio* on WSKV-FM. ETHAN MOORE

Oldfield basically runs the store for ninety minutes, jotting down phone numbers and reading texts as quickly as they come in.

The station slogan is "Pickup Country," and you never know what you might be able to pick up. "Livestock and garden plants are big in the spring," Oldfield said. "In the fall, there are a lot of calls for firewood."

Listeners heard these pitches in rapid succession:

- "I have for sale this morning a hearing aid."
- "I've got an ungodly amount of junk I need to get rid of. I'm sure I have something somebody needs."
- "I have some old-time postcards I'd like to sell."
- "I have some Elvis DVD movies I'll sell for four dollars apiece."
- "I've got a chicken coop for sale, the little fancy kind."
- "My friend has a water heater still in the box she would like to sell."

Tradio streams online, and the station is able to track where listeners are located. Surprisingly, people tune in from all over the world—fans who have no intention of buying anything from a seller in a small town in Kentucky.

"I think many of them are people who used to live here and like to hear voices or accents they recognize," Oldfield said.

Station manager Ethan Moore said, "We've actually verified that service members are listening from military bases. That's really neat because they're looking for a touch of home."

Moore and Oldfield take turns behind the microphone when *Tradio* is on the air, dividing up shifts during the week. He said they average more than one hundred calls each day. The show used to be on for one hour a day, five days a week. They found listeners wanted more. So a few years ago, they expanded it to ninety minutes a day, Monday through Saturday. That is 468 hours of wheeling and dealing each year.

The hosts know some people would listen all day every day if they kept the phone lines open. "If you want to get your ad on, you'd better make it quick," Oldfield said as the clock neared 11:30 a.m.

She still laughs about a call she got not long after she started hosting the show. A caller said he had a bag of body parts he needed to get rid of. "The way he was talking kind of scared me, and I was getting ready to call the police," she said. But after he talked a little longer, it became clear that he was describing parts for a dirt bike!

Radio formats change all the time, but WSKV has no plans to drop its most popular show. "They'd be out here at our front door, banging on it and shouting, 'Bring *Tradio* back,'" Oldfield laughed.

Tradio connects people who know each other by voice and love the sound of a good bargain.

When Oldfield signs off, again, it is as if she is talking to her closest friends. "You guys be blessed and remember I love y'all . . . and there ain't nothing you can do about it!"

CALLS FROM HOME

WHITESBURG

It is not unusual for a radio disc jockey to take song requests. What is unusual is who is making the requests on Monday nights at WMMT-FM in Whitesburg.

While Gabby Gillespie is on the air with a show called *Hip Hop from the Hilltop*, Elizabeth Sanders is in another room, recording the requests and some very personalized messages. The shout-outs come from people who have loved ones incarcerated in one of the seven state or federal prisons within the listening area. Those messages will be played back after the hip-hop show.

The calls come from cities all along the East Coast of the United States and sometimes from as far away as Hawaii or the U.S. Virgin Islands. Nearly

Gabby Gillespie hosts a popular hip-hop radio show at WMMT-FM.

five thousand people are locked up in the nearby prisons in eastern Kentucky, southwestern Virginia, and southern West Virginia.

While other parts of the country have a "not in my backyard" attitude toward prisons, elected leaders welcome prisons in this region as a form of economic development, hoping to offset the loss of thousands of coal mining jobs.

The show is called *Calls from Home*, and the messages are a once-a-week connection for many families.

The messages come from mothers and wives who are trying to keep their sons and husbands in the loop about the life events they are missing:

- "Lilly had to run a race with her group at school, and she finished and got a little medal."
- "I'm hanging in here, trying to find a way to pay the rent."
- "I ate a little kiwi for breakfast, trying to stay healthy."
- "Keep your head up and keep your faith. Love you son."

Family members often can't get to central Appalachia to visit their loved ones who are behind bars. "We don't have great public transportation here in the mountains," Sanders said, outlining the challenges. "It's limited if you don't have a car or the time you need to get here, the hours it takes. You have to have a place to stay and take off work. It's rough."

"It can be heart-wrenching to hear some of the calls, but it also brings a lot of joy," said Gillespie.

Calls from Home began in the early 2000s almost by accident when a family member of an inmate in Virginia's Red Onion Prison called in and asked to give a shout-out to her loved one over the air. She knew the inmate listened to the station's hip-hop show. The disc jockey on duty allowed it and soon realized a lot of inmates were tuning in. WMMT is a listener-supported public radio station dedicated to being the voice of mountain people's music, culture, and social issues. It produces documentaries about the region and plays a wide variety of music from hip-hop to bluegrass, country, and gospel.

WMMT is part of Appalshop, a renowned nonprofit arts and filmmaking center. *Calls from Home* perfectly fits its mission of documenting Appalachian culture and challenging stereotypes. The station now has binders full of thank-you letters from inmates and their family members.

The shout-outs are usually quite simple. It is all about hearing a friendly voice. But sometimes the news is sad. Callers have reported deaths in the family or ended a relationship. Children tell dads they wish they could come to school events.

"In an ideal situation, it wouldn't be me recording," Sanders said. "They'd be able to talk directly to their loved one, and it wouldn't have to air out for everyone to hear."

Getting phone calls in and out of a prison can be difficult and expensive, so the audio board lights up when the station's toll-free line opens. Sanders said it is somewhat surprising that there have been very few complaints about the show. Listeners seem to accept it as a public service.

"A lot of people ignore folks who are locked up," said Gillespie. "And you know, they're as much a part of this community as anyone else in our eyes."

Sometimes the messages aren't meant to be private.

For example, a grandmother from Roanoke, Virginia, intends for her words to reach not only her grandson but also his fellow inmates and the law-abiding citizens who are tuned in. On one call, she said, "If we learn to treat each other like we love ourselves, the way we want to be treated, oh, what a great world this would be."

LARKSPUR PRESS

MONTEREY

In a workshop in rural Owen County, Gray Zeitz minds his p's and q's.

"I guess it helps if you're a little bit dyslexic because everything is backward," he said.

The scholarly-looking man with the white beard spends several hours each day placing metal type into rows, forming words one letter at a time that become sentences, then paragraphs, then chapters. He must look at the letters upside down and backward as he places them into trays.

"I've done it so long, sometimes when I'm writing I have to stop and think which way a *b* or a *d* goes," he said. Since 1974, Zeitz has operated

Gray Zeitz patiently places metal letters in a tray to form lines of type at Larkspur Press.

Gray Zeitz sits in his office at Larkspur Press, surrounded by books he has produced and linen-like paper that will be used in his print shop.

Larkspur Press, a small business that prints books the old-fashioned way. He got interested in this style of printing while attending the University of Kentucky. He said he saw a hand press on display at King Library Press. "After that, I was hooked," he said. He got an apprenticeship there to learn the process and started his own literary magazine.

"The press I'm using now was built in 1916, and setting type goes all the way back to Johannes Gutenberg," he said. The German craftsman invented the printing press in the mid-1400s.

Life moves at a slower pace at Larkspur Press, which is in a building that sits in a field along a creek. Zeitz can watch birds come to feeders outside the windows as he drops the metal letters in place, or he can see an occasional deer. For hours at a time, he may be the only person in the shop.

"People come in and say, 'Oh, I could never do this,'" Zeitz said. But he likes the solitude that comes with a job that requires patience and tremendous attention to detail. "You can't feel pressure. When you are forced to work fast, that only makes you have more mistakes."

"Clink, clink, clink," the letters and spacers fall into line. It is the same sound you would have heard in a print shop in the fifteenth century.

Larkspur Press releases just two or three books a year, mostly poetry and short fiction by Kentucky authors. They are collectible because of their scarcity. Among the authors featured are Wendell Berry, James Baker Hall, Thomas Merton, and Bobbie Ann Mason. He prints only books he likes by authors he knows.

The books are printed on handmade paper that almost feels like fabric.

"They have the work of the hand in them," Zeitz said. "That really just says it. You can tell it was handmade." He has one coworker, Leslie Shane, who comes in a few days a month. Her job is slow, too. She sews the pages into the books.

The bookmaker said he doesn't know of another press in the country that does what he does, which is turn out handmade editions of three hundred to six hundred copies that are affordable. Most of his books sell for $20 to $40. Other hand presses may do only large special editions that can cost hundreds of dollars. Larkspur has done a few of those, too, and, at the other extreme, illustrated note cards.

"I print letterpress because I enjoy it and I think it looks better," Zeitz said.

The press is the only motorized thing in the print shop, and when Zeitz is feeding pages into it by hand, it is the only part of the process that has a steady pace. "It's a dance, just a dance," he said as he placed pages one at a time into the antique machine. The press clamps tight, squeezing the paper and the inked type together to make a printed page. He adds a dab of ink to the press every thirty-five sheets. A page goes through the press twice so it can be printed on both sides. The finished product is a work of art.

Zeitz doesn't do much by computer. Larkspur Press does have a website, but it is managed by a friend. There are no online sales and not much of an advertising budget, just a mailing list for sending announcements to booksellers and past customers. The books are found in independent bookstores throughout the state.

Zeitz said he is always about two years behind schedule.

"Clink, clink, clink."

He may never catch up, and that is fine with him. "I enjoy every part of it. There's a lot to be said about having a job you enjoy."

THOROUGHBREDS FOR SALE

LEXINGTON

Each October, crowds pack into Keeneland race course to take in the fall meet. More than twenty thousand people show up on some days for food and fashion, bourbon and betting. Many horse racing fans believe the Lexington course is the most beautiful racetrack in the world. A month before the fall meet, another event can be just as riveting as the races, but many people are not aware it is open to the public.

The September Yearling Sale is the biggest auction of its kind anywhere, with more than four thousand Thoroughbreds being sold over two weeks. Buyers come from all over the United States and elsewhere, such as France, Dubai, and Saudi Arabia. Observers are surrounded by wealth, and watching the bidding is like attending the theater. It is high drama as prices soar into the hundreds of thousands of dollars.

Auctioneer Ryan Mahan said you never know what to expect, "especially if you get two guys with a lot of money and maybe a little ego." He said when each bidder is determined to get the last word, a horse that was expected to sell for $200,000 might end up at $600,000 or $700,000.

"That's the blue sky we look for in the horse business," Mahan said. "You never really know what will happen when the captains of the industry get in these seats. They don't like to lose."

If the buyers believe they are looking at a future Kentucky Derby winner in the auction ring, the atmosphere in the room changes.

"When one of them begins to creep past the million-dollar mark, you can tell a hush sort of comes over the arena, and people are really watching to see what's next, how high it's going to go," said Amy Gregory, Keeneland's communications director.

It is not unusual to see a colt sell for $1 million or more at the Keeneland September Yearling Sale. KEENELAND PHOTO

The sales pavilion is not a typical livestock auction barn. The horses are escorted to the sales ring on padded walkways by handlers dressed in suits and ties. The walls outside the arena are covered with fine art, mostly depicting race scenes. It is a spotless venue, not caked in mud and manure.

If you are not a registered buyer, you can sit on benches just outside the arena and watch through windows. Anyone can hear the bidding through speakers mounted in the ceiling.

Most of the bid spotters have worked in the same sections of the room for years and know the buyers who have their own marked seats. There is not much danger that spectators will be mistaken for bidders if they scratch their noses or nod their heads. "There are stories, though, of people saying,

'I didn't really bid on that horse, but I was embarrassed not to sign the ticket,'" Mahan said. "You have to be wealthy to do that!"

Mahan said he has seen instances when an unintentional buyer got a horse for perhaps $40,000 and ended up winning $300,000 when it made it to the track. But that works both ways, with expensive horses sometimes never winning a dime.

Just like in the race day grandstand, the sales pavilion is a place for good food and great people watching. Bob Elliston, vice president of sales, said, "If you've got a passing interest or a casual interest in horse racing, you've seen the Kentucky Derby and know who the top trainers are, like Bob Baffert or D. Wayne Lucas. Here, one of them may be sitting right next to you or may walk by you."

Keeneland also has a sale for horses of all ages in January and a breeding stock sale in November. Those auctions are also open to the public. The track wants more people to consider the sales as a tourist attraction.

Watching the horse sales at Keeneland can be an entertaining and educational experience for spectators. KEENELAND PHOTO

More than four thousand Thoroughbreds are sold at Keeneland each September.
KENTUCKY TOURISM

In September 2017, a family from Florida and Louisiana found themselves in Lexington after fleeing Hurricane Irma. They decided to check out the horse sales as they waited to hear it was safe to go back home. They gasped in amazement when they watched three horses sell for more than $2 million each.

"We thought we might as well make a family experience out of it and not let the hurricane stop us from having fun," said Naomi Cohn of Baton Rouge. "We heard about the horse sale, and this is probably one of the most fascinating things we've ever seen."

Yes, the sales are fascinating and perhaps a glimpse into the future. The horse that walks past you today may run for the roses two years from now.

RACETRACK SUPERSTITIONS

LEXINGTON

A horse racetrack is a place for people watching, full of tradition, ambition, and superstition. Most of the people who come through the gates at the many tracks in Kentucky hope to get lucky. Race fans, trainers, and jockeys all have their perceived formulas for success and practices to avoid.

Kaleigh Binkley of Elizabethtown, a frequent visitor to Keeneland, spends much of her time looking down as she walks through the paddock area and grandstand. She believes if she can find a penny with heads up, that is an omen she is going to have a profitable day at the betting windows.

Some bettors won't select a horse until they've seen them in the paddock. If they discover there is only one gray horse in a race, they have to bet it. They want to go for the horse that stands out in the crowd. Garry Welsh of Winchester said he always wants to see the horses first because it gives him an idea of their mindset. "If they're frisky and bouncing around, that's my horse," he said.

One common superstition is that you should avoid betting on a horse with four white "socks." One white leg is considered to be good, two or three is okay, but four is a no-no. That didn't hold true for California Chrome, a Thoroughbred with four white ankles that won the 2014 Kentucky Derby and Preakness.

For other bettors, size matters, and colors count. "I think you bet on the shortest jockey or any jockey who is wearing pink," said Brooke Murphy from Kenton County.

Of course, there are those who study the records, trying to make informed choices based on a horse's lifetime earnings and recent performances. They're locked in to statistics instead of colors or names. But there is superstition in that approach, too. Many people making their picks believe it's bad luck to let someone buy their racing program or share it.

Numbers often come into play. "I do not pick any unlucky numbers for me," said Alexis Warren, who avoids two, four, six, and eight. "I just don't like even numbers."

"Number five is always the one I have to bet, and then I have to go to the same betting clerk or window every time I make my bet," said Lisa Mitchell of Cleveland, Ohio. That is a common belief among bettors. If you win a race, you don't want to mess with fate. Many believe going to a different betting window or machine is a sure way to break your streak. Some people also believe you should hold on to winning tickets and cash all of them at the end of the day.

The superstitions carry beyond the grandstand and betting windows. No horse at Keeneland must be stabled in Barn 13 because a barn with that unlucky number doesn't exist. Many trainers believe it is bad luck to keep a broom in a stable, and if they hang a horseshoe in a stall, it must be with the ends up so that the luck won't run out.

Almost every jockey will admit to having superstitions. Perhaps the most common one is to not change a piece of apparel if they're having a

There is no "unlucky" Barn 13 at Keeneland.

good week, maybe wearing the same riding pants or boots for several days in a row.

"I know there was one meet at Turfway Park where I was really having a good week," said retired jockey Patti Cooksey. She's the second-winningest female rider of all time. "I wore the same underwear every single day," she laughed. "It got washed every night, but, if it's going well, you don't want to break the routine."

Jockeys also feel encouraged or deflated depending on what gate they will be starting from in a race. They are assigned through a random draw. For the Kentucky Derby at Churchill Downs, jockeys cross their fingers, hoping to avoid the number seventeen position on draw day. No horse has ever won the derby from that gate. Gate five has the best record for winners.

There are as many superstitions as there are betting combinations. Raven Cox of Atlanta said she can't stand on the far-right side of the track when she visits Keeneland. That's a bad-luck location in her mind.

"BETologists" at Keeneland—experts who teach newcomers how to bet—see a lot of people going through good luck rituals. Some truly carry a rabbit's foot or four-leaf clover in their pocket or wallet. BETologist Jack Peffer said if he gives advice to someone and they win, he often sees them back before every race. They treat him like a good-luck charm.

"Back in the 1970s and 1980s, $2 bills were more common," Peffer said. "You would have thought that would've been perfect to use for a $2 bet, but a lot of bettors thought they were bad luck." Some racegoers also refuse to break a $50 bill. The reasons are unclear. It is just one of those things people have heard they shouldn't do.

You will also hear trainers say it is bad luck to eat peanuts at the track, and you won't find them for sale anywhere on the grounds. Perhaps it's because if a horse stepped on a shell, it could get caught in its hoof and affect the way it walks or runs.

No doubt about it, some racegoers seem to have an inside track to winning, while a dark cloud hangs over others. There is something magical about the beautiful racetracks in Kentucky. They're charming, and so are many of the rituals that take place on race day, from start to finish.

PRIMATE RESCUE CENTER

JESSAMINE COUNTY

The Primate Rescue Center has been tucked away on private land near Nicholasville for more than thirty years, yet many central Kentuckians have never heard of it. That is because it is truly a sanctuary, not a zoo or tourist attraction.

The population of monkeys and chimpanzees stays around fifty. The primates ended up on the thirty-acre farm after spending years in medical research labs, the entertainment industry, or private homes. In many cases, the primates were confiscated by wildlife officers in states where it is illegal to keep them.

The Primate Rescue Center was founded in the late 1980s, when Clay Miller gave his future wife, April Truitt, a macaque as a pet. The couple soon realized the young monkey needed a companion of his own species. "As they investigated the industry, they realized there were a lot of monkeys out there that were purchased as babies that quickly outgrew that cute diaper-wearing, bottle-fed stage and became wild animals in people's homes," said Eileen Dunnington Dallaire, the center's executive director. They discovered many cases of monkeys seriously injuring their owners and others.

So Truitt and Miller made it their mission to make a difference and end the suffering experienced by many primates. They built a monkey haven, a place where the primates are no longer on display, where they can interact with each other and live in an environment that is as natural as they can make it in Kentucky.

"We know we can't re-create the wild in captivity," Dallaire said. "But we can provide enrichment, good nutrition, medical care, and all the necessary elements that will give them good lives."

Dozens of primates, including this chimp, are cared for at a sanctuary in Jessamine County. PRIMATE RESCUE CENTER

She said, "Our mission is to offer them the peace and calm that is sanctuary." That is why the facility is open to the public just one day a year, only to donors with an invitation.

"We hope the public is able to learn about the primates through other avenues, such as social media and our website, in order to fall in love with them and want to support them," Dallaire said.

She became the center's executive director in 2018 after Truitt retired, but Dallaire was not a newcomer to the mission. She came to work at the rescue center fourteen years before that, first as a volunteer and later as a caregiver. "Once you come here and experience these guys' lives and personalities, it's really difficult not to want to help and to give back to them," she said.

Jessamine County becomes the permanent home for the monkeys and apes. They will retire at the center. A chimpanzee can live to be sixty-five, so caring for one can be a long-term commitment.

"That's a lot of pounds of produce and a lot of enrichment toys and medical care," Dallaire said. "All of that is quite expensive."

The centerpiece of the sanctuary is a large chimpanzee enclosure, filled with climbing structures designed to make the residents feel at home. A tunnel allows the chimps to move freely between the outdoor space and a temperature-controlled sleeping area and playroom. There are also ten other indoor/outdoor enclosures for monkeys.

The budget is about a half million dollars a year for the tax-exempt, nonprofit organization, which gets its entire funding from private donations. It gets no money from the state or federal governments. It relies on dedicated employees and volunteers who feed the animals, clean their enclosures, and maintain their toys and exercise equipment. On an average day, the staff and volunteers process three hundred pounds of fresh fruits, vegetables, nuts, and grains to serve to the primates.

"These apes and monkeys don't have the skills to be reintroduced into the wild," Dallaire said. "We are able to offer them lifetime care to live out the rest of their days." They live those golden years far from their native jungles, among maple trees and fields of bluegrass, getting a daily dose of Kentucky hospitality.

DIPPIN' DOTS

PADUCAH

Natives believe Kentucky is a pretty cool place. It is also home to one of the coldest products on the planet.

The Dippin' Dots factory in Paducah looks like a mad scientist's lab. It is a place where it snows indoors, machinery is covered in ice, and foggy vapor comes out of bags and boxes.

In 1988, Curt Jones, a microbiologist working at Alltech in Lexington, was experimenting with a flash-freezing process while trying to find a way

More than 2 billion Dippin' Dots are made each day at a factory in Paducah.

DIPPIN' DOTS

An employee fills a bag with Dippin' Dots as they come from a frost-covered processing machine. DIPPIN' DOTS

to make livestock feed more efficient. He discovered that the feed would turn into small pellets when exposed to liquid nitrogen at a temperature of −320°F. As an ice cream lover, he played around with the process some more and loved how it instantly turned cream into beads.

Stan Jones, who is not related to Curt, has been the chief development officer at Dippin' Dots since the beginning. He said, "Curt showed up in my office with a sample of the beads and wanted to know what I thought about it. I said, 'You might have something here. It's kind of different.'"

Curt Jones started making the extreme ice cream in his parents' garage in Illinois, selling it at fairs and festivals out of portable coolers packed with dry ice. One year after the invention of Dippin' Dots, Opryland USA in Nashville signed on as the first amusement park to offer the treat.

Because the dots need to be stored in super cold conditions to keep their consistency, it became clear that working from a garage wasn't going to work for long. When Curt Jones began to line up more customers, he had to find a facility where he had more room for production and storage. So he moved the operation to a building across the Ohio River in Paducah.

Now, nearly forty years later, the little dots are a big deal, with annual retail sales of $300 million. The plant has been expanded three times. Dippin' Dots are sold at theme parks, malls, zoos, aquariums, and two-thirds of all baseball stadiums in the country as well as some convenience stores that have special Dippin' Dots freezers.

Here's the scoop: The factory now turns out more than 2 billion dots a day that can be made into seventy flavors. Chocolate is the best seller, followed by cookies and cream. Nontraditional flavors include banana split, brownie batter, and strawberry cheesecake.

All Dippin' Dots sold in the United States are made in Paducah, and they're also shipped from Kentucky to seven other countries. "We were the original," Stan Jones said. "We've been doing it longer than anyone else. Anyone with a beaded product is going from our lead."

In 1995, Dippin' Dots made its international debut in Japan, marketed as the "Ice Cream of the Future."

If you walk through the production room, it looks as if you've entered the Arctic Circle. Employees are covered from head to toe in white uniforms and wear rubber gloves. Frozen dots move from the processing tanks, fall from frost-covered tubes into plastic bags, and move down the production line to be boxed. But it is actually 70°F in the main room. The combination of a warm room and a super cold product keeps the plant covered in a fog. It is a different story in the storage room, which is kept at −47°F. When that door is opened, the moisture in the air instantly turns to snow, and you can see flakes fall to the floor. Employees can't stay in there more than two or three minutes.

Dippin' Dots has had its ups and downs, nearly going bankrupt in 2011. The company was purchased by Fischer Enterprises, a family-owned operation that brought new marketing strategies to the business that led to a rebound. It also added Doc Popcorn to its product line. The company was sold again in 2022 to J&J Snack Foods.

The flash-frozen ice cream is now sold in 22,000 venues, with an expanded focus on home deliveries. Fans can order Dippin' Dots online and have their favorite flavors arrive on their doorstep, packed in dry ice. There's a catch, though. The dots must be consumed the day they arrive, or the dry ice in the packaging must be replenished. Home freezers aren't cold enough for storing the product.

Dippin' Dots recently expanded into China. Stan Jones said, "It looks like a very big market. We think it will pass the U.S. market in a short time, so we're excited about that." No matter where the company goes from here, executives will always be proud of its Kentucky roots, telling the story of how one man's curiosity about the cold turned into a sweet treat to beat the heat.

DEAD FRED

DANVILLE

College football fans love their game-day traditions. At Tennessee, the band plays "Rocky Top," Georgia fans bring a bulldog onto the field, and Kentucky's Wildcat mascot does push-ups each time the team scores. But Centre College, a small liberal arts institution in Danville, may have one of the most unusual traditions.

At each home football game, a large portrait is carried into the Colonels' stadium by members of the Phi Delta Theta fraternity. Fans acknowledge the painting as it passes and makes its way into the stands, with many shouting with glee, "Fred is here!"

A portrait of Fred Vinson gets passed around as members of the Phi Delta Theta fraternity enjoy a football game at Centre College in October 2016.

It is a portrait of Fred M. Vinson, a member of the fraternity who was a three-sport athlete in baseball, basketball, and football while studying at Centre. Vinson went on to represent Kentucky as a U.S. congressman for six terms. President Harry S. Truman appointed him to be the nation's treasury secretary in 1945 and the next year nominated him to become chief justice of the U.S. Supreme Court. Vinson held that position until his death in 1953.

In 2016, student Chandler Sneed recited the highlights of Vinson's bio to me, proving that every Phi Delt is well-versed in the accomplishments of the famous graduate. "Fred Vinson was a very significant student," Sneed said. "He graduated in 1909 at the top of his class and had the opportunity to play professional baseball, but he turned that down to pursue law."

Vinson's portrait is displayed prominently in the fraternity house, where he is affectionately known as "Dead Fred." But it doesn't just hang around. The portrait has been the centerpiece of an off-the-wall game-day tradition for more than a half century.

"When he was alive, he never missed a game, and we never want him to miss a game now," said fraternity member Max Mazza.

Sometimes, there are just a couple brothers who can take the portrait to tailgate parties and other pregame activities. Seventy-five percent of the Phi Delts are tied up before the game because they are on the football team.

The portrait gets propped up in the tailgate area for an hour or two on home-game Saturdays, where Dead Fred appears to watch people pass while he is behind glass. Then someone sounds a horn, signaling it is almost time for kickoff. Fred gets a lift to the stadium. Fans file behind his escorts as he makes his entrance. Throughout the game, the portrait is passed around and raised above heads as the fans cheer on their team.

David Bettis was a Phi Delt when the tradition started. "I try to come back every year," he said. "And I expect Dead Fred at the games. He needs to be there."

"The first guy who thought to take Fred M. Vinson to a football game was this fellow right here," Bettis said, pointing to a picture of Mike Dyer in the 1967 composite photo on the frat house wall. He remembers they did it on a whim, taking the portrait off campus to a game in Indiana just to show off their famous brother.

"I questioned it at the time, but because Mike was an upperclassman, I thought if that's what the guys wanted to do, it was okay," Bettis said.

The portrait never goes off campus now but does show up at other big events. In 2000, Centre College hosted the U.S. vice-presidential debate, becoming the smallest college in the smallest town to ever do so. The lively match between Dick Cheney and Joe Lieberman was dubbed the "Thrill in the Ville." The portrait of Dead Fred had a seat in the gallery. It went so well that the college hosted the vice-presidential candidates again in 2012, when incumbent Joe Biden debated Paul Ryan. Again, Dead Fred was there.

"We see him as a good-luck charm, and we're going to keep that going," Sneed said. "I hope he would appreciate it and like it. I'm sure he'd be glad that he's contributing to what we do today."

The Centre Colonels win a lot more home football games than they lose, competing in NCAA Division III. There is no way to know if the team would perform differently without Fred's attendance, but he certainly provides the framework for a lot of fun.

THE MARBLE CLUB
SUPER DOME

TOMPKINSVILLE

A weather-beaten shack in a field may not look like much from the outside, but in Monroe County, it is a premier sports arena known as the Marble Club Super Dome.

It is a place where grown men get down and dirty and play a game called rolley hole, which is sort of like croquet. Players try to get their marble in a hole and knock opponents out of contention.

"It's a great game," said veteran player Jack Head. "You've got defense, offense, strategy—the whole shot right there."

Rolley hole is played on a dirt floor in the Marble Club Super Dome in Tompkinsville.

The dome has been a hangout since 1988, when several of the players got together and built it as a place where they could compete year-round. Before that, most of their matches were played outdoors in marble yards.

Folks have been playing marbles around Tompkinsville for decades, and the club has always been a source of pride. "We used to have more than a hundred members," said regular player Billy Emberton. But numbers have dwindled as people moved away and younger people have found other pastimes.

Emberton said he lives in the marble capital of the world. "They used to say it was Moss, Tennessee, but I believe it's Monroe County now," he said.

Moss is just across the border in Clay County, Tennessee, where a national tournament takes place each September at Standing Stone State Park. So many of the Monroe County players have come back with prizes and titles over the years that club members have lost count.

The players treasure their marbles, handmade from squares of flint. Glass marbles would chip and shatter from the hard hits they would take in rolley hole. Billy's brother, Robert Emberton, said a good marble can sell for anywhere from $15 to $80.

"You don't want to lose them," he said. "Some people can make one in two hours. It would take me two weeks." Each player has their favorite marbles, ones they believe bring them good luck.

Robert was part of a team of sharpshooters from Kentucky and Tennessee that was invited to the British Marbles Championship in London in 1992. The Americans played a more traditional game there, with a goal of knocking other marbles out of a ring. It wasn't rolley hole, but their shooting skills bested the British in seven consecutive matches. They became the first overseas team to win the overall trophy in the four-hundred-year history of that tournament.

Some of the guys who are in their seventies and eighties have been playing marbles for as long as they can remember but know if they want to keep the tradition alive, they need to get some younger players interested.

Billy's grandson, Dylan Emberton, is in his twenties and tries to recruit fresh players from among his peers. "It's kind of hard nowadays with all the technology and stuff," he said. But he said rolley hole should appeal to young athletes.

"You get your exercise out here, getting up and down, crawling around on the floor," he said. "You know, you always want to win, and this is where you can do it."

It is a tight-knit club with just a handful of members, but it is not exclusive. The doors are open to anyone. On most nights, there are a few spectators sitting on benches around the wood-burning stove or whittling on a stick while the marbles clink and fly across the dirt floor.

"We like for people to come watch us," Billy said. "We're proud of our game."

They welcome anyone who wants to learn the rules, and even though most nights it seems like a men's club, women are invited to play, too. Members said they have had some extremely competitive female players in the past.

The games may look like child's play, but the veteran players have been hooked for life, hoping that generations from now, people will still come to the Dome to let the good times roll.

HOME FOR WAYWARD BABYDOLLS

ELLIOTTVILLE

From the moment you step onto the lawn of a certain home in rural Rowan County, you may feel you are being watched. Eyes peer at you from trees, fence posts, flower beds, and even clear cases embedded in the sidewalk. The homeowner will greet you by declaring his credentials: "I'm very pleased to have been awarded the title of slightly mad scientist."

Cecil Ison is the self-appointed lead researcher at the Home for Wayward Babydolls. "Any doll abandoned, abused, no matter what type of condition they're in, they're welcome here to spend out their last days," he said.

Cecil is a retired forest ranger and archaeologist. In the mid-1980s, he began collecting dolls he found in the woods, and, surprisingly, there were a lot of them.

"It was just too interesting to look at another side of human behavior, and that was the abuse of babydolls," he said.

He found discarded dolls that had been shot, stabbed, burned, and decapitated. He just couldn't leave them alone in the wilderness, saying they were manufactured to be loved. He took them to his office and, on retirement in 2005, brought them home.

Now, with tongue in cheek, Cecil maintains his research facilities, along with his wife, Bet, the home's "executive director." He calls himself a "forensic anthropomorphologist," also known as a studier of abused babydolls.

One outbuilding holds containers stacked to the ceiling filled with dolls that have been donated, left at their doorstep, or arrived by mail. Bet labels each box, documenting the contents.

Cecil Ison sits on the porch at his Home for Wayward Babydolls in Rowan County, a "sanctuary" for abandoned dolls and mannequins. LIBRARY OF CONGRESS, PHOTOGRAPH BY CAROL M. HIGHSMITH, LC-DIG-HIGHSM-64118

A fenced-in area near the road is dubbed "Research Area 14-C." It is devoted to the study of Barbies and "Barbie wannabes," which are tied to planks to endure heat, rain, and snow. Cecil has noted that real Barbies stand up to the weather elements much better than the copycats.

In a tobacco barn, dolls hang from the rafters, many of them muddy and missing limbs. "These are all crime scene victims," Cecil said.

Bet has also rescued larger doll-like figures—mannequins that came from closed department stores. They sit on the porch, and she changes their clothing with the seasons. "Normally, we don't have to decorate much for Halloween," she said. "It's already here."

In fact, that is what all the dolls are—decorations. Some people might call the whole property a work of folk art. "I just call it the way we live," Cecil said.

They display toys where others might have a birdbath or pink flamingo. Found Furbys stand in a line near the porch. Plastic trolls hide along a path near the barn.

"We decorate with what we have and, fortunately for us, we have lots of babydolls," Bet said. They also have colorful murals on the side of their house and storage sheds that they have made with thousands of bottle caps and brightly painted gourds that hang on the porch.

The Isons realize some people think it is creepy to see dolls hanging in trees or sitting in birdcages and to walk down paths lined with plastic heads pegged to fence posts. To them, it is just watching what nature can create through the natural process of decay.

Now dolls come to them from all over the world. Hunters bring them to the Isons after finding them in the woods. Trash collectors rescue them from dumpsters. Thrift store managers have donated dolls they couldn't sell.

"In the height of the clown scare, a lady brought us a whole box of clown heads," Bet said. In an outbuilding called "Curation Facility Number One," there is a shelf that holds boxed dolls purported to be haunted or possessed. If visitors want to go near them, Cecil provides them with a lead vest for some extra protection.

A doll is attached to a fence outside the Home for Wayward Babydolls, one of hundreds that populate the property.

"I don't question them. I just record the claims as they come in," he said.

So what do the neighbors think about living close to the curious and conspicuous collection? "All of our neighbors are relatives," Bet said. "They think, 'Oh, that's just Cecil. He's always been that way!'"

It is not easy to describe the Home for Wayward Babydolls. It is not an official tourist attraction or museum listed in brochures. It is a private residence, and the best way to see the collection and new additions is to follow it on Facebook. And despite what Cecil says, it is not a real active center for scientific discovery.

"I still dabble in research, but for the most part now, we're a refuge," he said.

It is a quirky sanctuary where the smiles on dolls may last for decades— home sweet home for a man, his wife, and their hundreds of babies.

Cecil simply said, "I hope it's just a happy place."

DISCO BATHROOMS

FLORENCE

Things are often hopping at HOP Shops in northern Kentucky, but the crowds of customers aren't there just to buy snacks or gas up their cars. They're curious about the big red buttons in the bathrooms.

A sign above the buttons just inside the doors clearly states, in capital letters, "Do Not Push." But underneath the words is a picture of the chain's mascot, Hopper the Frog. He is winking, implying that the rule is meant to be broken.

Mary Moss, the manager at HOP Shops in Walton, said people often come out of the bathroom and tell her they resisted pushing the button

The bathrooms at HOP Shops become a disco with the push of a button.

even though they were tempted. She tells them to go back in. "We want you to push it!" she says.

One push sets in motion mirrored disco balls mounted on the ceiling. The main light goes off, and colored spotlights come on, sending thousands of spots spinning across the walls and stalls, ceiling and sinks. A song from the disco era comes through a speaker. At the Walton store, patrons hear "I've Had the Time of My Life" from the *Dirty Dancing* soundtrack. At the Florence store on Mount Zion Road, Bruce Springsteen belts out "Dancing in the Dark."

Customers usually burst into laughter and pull out their mobile phones to record a video.

HOP Shops are owned and operated by Valor Oil, a company based in Owensboro, Kentucky. The company entered the convenience store business in 2018 after buying HOP Shops from another oil company.

Ann Gilbert, Valor Oil's manager of human resources, said the company's vice president of retail marketing, Damon Bail, gets credit for the quirky idea of turning the stores' bathrooms into tiny dance spaces.

"He was trying to figure out something that would make us a destination," Gilbert said. "One day, he told us he saw something about a disco bathroom in Canada. We liked the idea but just thought it would probably cost too much."

But Bail wouldn't give up. He found a contractor who figured out how to make it happen for what the company considered a reasonable price. The first disco bathrooms opened in February 2023 at a store just off Interstate 71 in Verona.

The bathrooms were an instant hit, with thousands of videos being shared on Facebook, TikTok, and Instagram. Gilbert said the company realized travelers have many choices for gas and snacks at interstate exits. It's good business to give people a good place to "do their business." After spending time in the bathroom, most people also spend some money at the checkout counter.

Within a year, six HOP Shops food marts had been renovated to include disco bathrooms. Five of them are in northern Kentucky; one is in Maineville, Ohio, near Kings Island Amusement Park. Gilbert is certain there will be many more.

Store managers say they see evidence all the time that people are seeking out the restrooms, sometimes driving out of their way to get to them. Moss said one tourist from Italy told her he was driving across the country and made it a point to map out a route that went past her store. "And I had a sixty-year-old woman who came out of the restroom and told me it was the best day of her life!" she said.

Alex Hudson of Florence may be the biggest fan of the flashy facilities. She celebrated her twentieth birthday by driving her friends to each disco bathroom. "They said, 'You want to do what for your birthday?'" she said. "I said, 'You heard me right. We're going to every HOP Shops location. They put a smile on my face!'" She has recorded dozens of TikTok videos showing a party in the potty.

Hudson said she often stops at the Florence HOP Shops before heading to morning classes at Thomas More University. "I just record a positive video and end it by pushing the red button. It's a good way to start my day."

HOP Shops have made a name for themselves as the place where you can boogie in the bathroom. Just know that when you're dancing in the dark, there's always the chance an unsuspecting visitor could open the door and wonder what's going on. You don't want to be caught with your pants down!

MORE TO ADORE

Kentucky is full of people who dance to a different drum—those who go full speed ahead with projects and ideas even when naysayers doubt them. When Howard Stratton and Grady Kinney came up with the idea for **Hillbilly Days** in 1977, a lot of people questioned the wisdom of perpetuating a stereotype of mountain people. But the cofounders of the Pikeville festival believed it was better to make fun of yourself than to let other people do it, and they saw it as a way to make a lot of money for Lexington's Shriners Children's Hospital.

The festival has grown into a joyous three-day event that draws 150,000 people each April to a city with a population of seven thousand. A parade features junk cars that look like the one the Clampetts drove on *The Beverly Hillbillies* television show in the 1960s. Floats feature moonshine stills, hound dogs, and gun-toting costumed characters with long beards, crooked teeth, and bare feet. It has grown into the second-largest festival in the state, surpassed only by the Kentucky Derby Festival in Louisville. The Shriners now have hillbilly clans in almost every state as well as Canada, and they present an annual check for $60,000 to $70,000 to the hospital.

Stratton said, "You can't take yourself too seriously. We're just good old country people who have a lot of fun." They also have big hearts.

Another annual event that draws a free-spirited crowd is the **World Chicken Festival** in London. One of the highlights of the four-day gathering each September is the Colonel Sanders Look-Alike Contest. Harland

Sanders perfected his recipe for Kentucky Fried Chicken at his café in nearby Corbin in the 1930s.

Men with goatees, dressed in white suits with string ties, try to mimic the colonel's walk and style of talk. Although taking the title onstage is something to crow about, most of the contestants stay in costume each day of the festival, roaming the grounds and posing for pictures.

"We like to call them our colonel ambassadors," said Kelly Burton, the contest coordinator. "A lot of them will take part in other contests throughout the week (such as the hot wings eating contest or the cornhole tournament). They'll mingle with the crowd, and who knows how many selfies they will be in?"

Another feature of the festival is the world's largest stainless-steel skillet, which can fry up to six hundred chicken quarters at once. It is another good place to get a glimpse of the counterfeit colonels.

The top prize for winning is $250, which doesn't cover the cost of travel for many of the look-alikes who come year after year from other states, such as Michigan, North Carolina, Tennessee, and West Virginia. But they don't do it for the money. It's the title that is on each one's bucket list.

᠎

It doesn't take long to notice a regular entry in Lexington parades marches outside the lines. The **March Madness Band** is the kind of troupe where members jump in where they can and let the rhythm overtake them. Music director Tripp Bratton, also known as the "Minister of Grooves," said the group is for people who loved being in a marching band in high school or college but maybe haven't picked up an instrument since. "Even if you have no experience, you can wave a flag or shake something," he said.

Seasoned musicians march alongside amateurs with the common goal of having fun. The band was meant to be a one-time thing, formed in 2008 to represent Local First Lexington, an alliance of small businesses, in the city's Christmas parade. But members enjoyed it so much that they couldn't give it up. The public loved it, too. Now the band sees it as its mission to add a little zaniness to any event it can be part of. The costumes are wild, the music is loud, and the choreography is crazy. Teresa Tomb, who heads the color guard and has the title "Minister of Moves," said it is a "whack-a-doodle stream of consciousness."

The band wants onlookers to know it's not just about what you can play but also about how playful you can be.

⁂

The skills of the Kent family seem limitless. The members are construction workers, sign hangers, and sound technicians as well as acrobats, magicians, and animal trainers. There are not many traveling circuses these days, and maybe none that is entirely made up of the members of one family.

The cast for this circus is Victor Kent; his wife, Mami; and four of their seven children. The former Californians relocated to the small town of Berea in 2016. Victor said the circus was getting a lot of bookings for fairs and festivals in the South and Midwest, and Kentucky seemed to be in the middle of the places they needed to go most often. "It didn't hurt that Kentucky is a comforting place. Every time we traveled here, we were just happy," he said.

The **Kent Family Magic Circus** is on the road for several months each year, but the team looks forward to downtime in Berea. It is time the siblings use to perfect their skills at juggling, learn new magic tricks, or devise more daring routines on the trapeze, turning their backyard into a training ground.

The only problem with this business model is that children grow up, move away, and start lives of their own. What does that mean for the future of the family circus? Victor said, while laughing, "There are always grandchildren!"

⁂

It took a leap of faith for Shaun and Julie Wendt to open a zoo in rural Nicholas County, forty-five minutes away from the nearest interstate. For twenty-five years, the couple and their three children have traveled to fairs and festivals with their mobile petting zoo. Their racing pigs were always

Two zebras are among the hundreds of animals on display at Wendt's Wildlife Adventure. JULIE WENDT

a big hit with the spectators on the midway. But Shaun said they just got tired of traveling. "We'd like to have the people come to us instead of us coming to the people."

They found a 125-acre farm near Carlisle, and Julie said, "It just seemed right." The farm is now licensed to house five hundred animals, from kangaroos to zebras, sloths, exotic birds, and camels. **Wendt's Wildlife Adventure** had become a tourist destination and a popular place for school field trips despite its out-of-the-way location. The property has a bonus attraction. Visitors can go inside a cabin that pioneer Daniel Boone built in 1795. It is the last place his family lived in Kentucky before moving on to Missouri.

༄

If you drive far enough south on Tates Creek Road in Lexington, you could be in for a surprise. The road ends abruptly at the Kentucky River.

But you don't have to turn around. Wait about three minutes, and the **Valley View Ferry** will be there to take you and your car into Madison County on the other side.

The ferry began operation in 1785, seven years before Kentucky became a state. That is why there is a Virginia flag flying from the front of the vessel alongside the U.S. and Kentucky flags. It is widely regarded to be the oldest continuously operating business in Kentucky. Some of the prominent people who have crossed on the ferry are Henry Clay, Daniel Boone, and Ulysses S. Grant.

Today, cars are carried across three at a time, with about fifteen thousand passengers taking the ferry each month. There is no toll to cross. The ferry is funded by the state transportation department and the governments of Fayette, Jessamine, and Madison counties, which have jointly owned it since 1991.

For some people, it is convenient to take the ferry; for others, it is a novelty, a leisurely way to take the road less traveled. The ferry generally operates from 6 a.m. to 6 p.m. on weekdays and from 8 a.m. to 8 p.m. on Saturdays and Sundays unless weather conditions prohibit it. Its operating status is kept up to date on the *Valley View Ferry* Facebook page.

Imagination reigns supreme at **Shannon Lamp Service** in Lexington. David Shannon carries on the business his father, Coleman Shannon, started in 1956. He and his wife, Amy, make handmade lampshades of any shape or size, with more than three thousand templates. David said a big-box store may stock just twenty to thirty sizes. So the little store in one of the city's older neighborhoods gets orders from all over the country.

But the store's real claim to fame is its reputation for being able to turn anything into a lamp. "We do a lot of porcelain vases, bourbon bottles, candlesticks, and figurines," David said. "But we also do unusual items, such as electric meters, fire extinguishers, roller skates, anything people bring in."

If you want a trophy or toy turned into a lamp, he can do it. If books turn you on, he can turn them on, as well as bait buckets, clocks, or bowling pins.

There is new life in an old motel just outside Beattyville. The former eyesore is now eye-catching. In late 2017, Dustin Cornett opened **Chocolat Inn and Café** in his hometown, providing luxury accommodations in an area known for campgrounds and cabins. "Many of the cabins in the Red River Gorge are great, but that's not for everyone," Cornett said. "Sometimes you want to come back to a room with a sixty-five-inch TV, high-speed internet, and a king-size mattress with plush pillows."

Cornett was one of those young people who wanted to get out of his small town and never look back. After he graduated from Western Kentucky University with a degree in broadcasting, he went on a six-year adventure to see the world. He liked bright lights and big cities. He met the woman who would become his wife while living in Japan, and much to his surprise, she fell in love with eastern Kentucky.

Mai Cornett said, "I love nature, and there is no stress here."

That taught her husband to love his hometown more and see business potential there. Dustin taught himself to roast coffee and make chocolates, using his grandmother's recipes, and Mai learned to make fancy pastries. But a coffee shop wouldn't be enough to make it in a town with fewer than two thousand residents, so they turned their attention to an old motel that was for sale. It was run down and had a bad reputation. It had been turned into apartments and looked like it hadn't been painted or repaired since the 1960s.

After nearly begging a banker to give him a chance, Dustin, at age thirty-one, got a loan and renovated the motel's eight rooms into luxury suites themed after places he had visited, such as Paris, Berlin, and Mumbai. The inn quickly picked up five-star reviews on travel sites, and hikers started coming from the gorge to get coffee, chocolates, and baked goods. "It helps that the nearest Starbucks is ninety miles away," Dustin laughed.

In 2023, the Cornetts sold the motel, now renamed the Three Rivers Inn, which retains the same commitment to quality. They moved to Rushville, Indiana, which is near where his grandmother lived (the one with the great chocolate recipes), because they saw a business opportunity. That town now has a Chocolat Café. But Dustin said he will always see Beattyville as the place that shaped him as an entrepreneur. He hopes his experience proves to others that it is not futile to dream big in a small place.

⟅⟆

Two other businesses near the Red River Gorge stand out for their unexpected *Spirit of the Bluegrass*. Miguel Ventura, an immigrant from Portugal, bought fifty acres in Slade, Kentucky, in 1983 and opened an ice cream shop in an abandoned store. Around that same time, the nearby gorge began to attract many rock climbers. The Venturas allowed many of them to camp on their property. The campers bought a little ice cream, but the Venturas soon realized there was a demand for real food. When they started making pizzas, business took off, with climbers and tourists lining up outside the door, sometimes waiting more than two hours for a pizza.

Miguel's Pizza has gained legendary status in the gorge. The restaurant provides a lot of summer jobs for the climbers who camp there for the whole season. Miguel's son, Dario, said the restaurant has never strayed from its commitment to making everything from the crust to the sauce from scratch. Customers can choose from nearly fifty toppings, with everything from mango salsa to tofu and sweet potatoes to pesto. "If you like corn on your pizza, we like it, too," Dario said.

The restaurant's logo, a smiling face with long, flowing hair, is also iconic. Dario said he has seen it on bumper stickers at campgrounds from coast to coast. He said Miguel's was a "poverty business at first" but is now a true example of the American dream, proof that you can start with nothing and, through hard work, make a good life for yourself even in remote places.

Another business that has taken off in the Red River Gorge region is **Turtle Farm Pottery** near Campton. Owner Casey Papendieck calls it a "magical place in the woods, where people are quietly making quality ceramic objects." He and his wife, Laura Gregory, met in Austin, Texas, and discovered the area after a rock-climbing trip to the gorge. "We didn't have any family here, and we didn't move here for jobs," Gregory said. "We really moved here just because we loved it."

Papendieck not only spins clay. He can spin tales of his life as a drifter. The Oregon native has been a street preacher, a migrant worker, a surfer, and a mountain climber. But now he is a master potter, with a degree from Berea College. Everyone who finds their way to Turtle Farm Pottery will find a three-person crew turning out beautiful mugs, bowls, and vases that are shipped around the world. If you're lucky, you may even get to hear the potters belt out a song. The couple is two-thirds of a quirky Americana band called the Handshake Deals.

Pottery is all about shaping things. Turtle Farm is shaping up to be just what the owners had hoped—a place where work and play go hand in hand.

ACKNOWLEDGMENTS

The challenge in writing a book like this is deciding what to leave out. This collection is just a third of the stories I have put together for my *Spirit of the Bluegrass* series, and more stories are being produced each month. Each person and place featured is worthy of recognition, but space limitations necessitate tough editing decisions. I am grateful to everyone who welcomes me into their homes or communities and allows me to tell their stories.

I want to thank many people who made this book possible. First, I am grateful to the general managers at WDKY-TV who have seen the value of this franchise and allowed me the freedom to travel as much or as far as I like to seek out stories. Ronna Corrente led the station when I first pitched the idea, and she embraced it. Jennifer Reiffer and Monte Costes followed and were just as supportive. News director Mark Glover has never once questioned what I'm up to when I say I have a "spirit shoot" or said a story had to be cut down even though I sometimes submit video pieces that are much longer than is the norm for a television newscast. I appreciate their trust and encouragement.

Former coanchors Erika Abe and Kristen Pflum were understanding when I was away from the news desk to travel or excused to do some last-minute editing while they held down the fort. Current coanchor Andrea Walker loves the series almost as much as I do and feeds me many ideas for stories. Thanks also to the management of our parent company, Nexstar Media Group, for allowing me to retell the stories here and share them with other stations in the corporate family.

I want to thank my editors, Greta Schmitz, Nicole Myers, Bruce Owens, and their team at Globe Pequot, for their enthusiasm and guidance throughout this process. It has been a pleasure to work with them.

Susan Thurman is a top-notch proofreader as well as a good friend. She graciously read my manuscript more than once and made corrections before I sent it to the publisher, making me look more skilled than I am. If you have questions about grammar, I recommend any of the style books she has written. I also want to thank Creighton Matthews, the go-to guy for graphics at WDKY. I am always peppering him with questions about design and layout.

My parents are gone now, but they deserve credit for instilling in me a love for exploring the world around me. My dad, who was a farmer and a school bus driver, knew every back road in Taylor County, West Virginia, where I grew up, and often took me, my mom, and my brother, Kevin, on Sunday drives to see things and meet the people along his route. We sat on a lot of porches and heard a lot of stories. Any time we were at a motel, restaurant, or rest stop with a brochure rack, my mother came away with a handful. She made sure we saw as many attractions as possible, both near our home and when away on vacations. I inherited that trait. When my in-laws travel with my immediate family now, they laughingly say they are prepared to "do it Bartlett-style," knowing we will pack in as many experiences as we can.

At the heart of it all, *Spirit of the Bluegrass* is about people who make us happy. For me, no one fills that role more than my wife, Elizabeth, and children, Cooper and Eliza.

You can see a video version of each story featured in this book on the *Spirit of the Bluegrass* YouTube channel: https://www.youtube.com/@SpiritoftheBluegrass.

The entire archive can be seen in a playlist on the FOX 56 News YouTube Channel: https://www.youtube.com/@FOX56News.

INDEX

ABOUT THE AUTHOR

Marvin Bartlett has worked in television news since 1985 and is the current anchor and managing editor for WDKY (FOX 56) in Lexington, Kentucky. He has been the anchor on this station from its beginning as a news operation in 1995. The "Spirit of the Bluegrass" franchise is entirely produced by Bartlett. He is the videographer, reporter, writer, and editor of the segments, a true "one-man band." Prior to that, Bartlett was a reporter/anchor for WLEX-TV in Lexington from 1987 to 1995. He was the eastern Kentucky bureau chief for WCHS-TV (Charleston, West Virginia) from 1985 to 1987. A native of Grafton, West Virginia, Bartlett graduated from Marshall University (1983) with a bachelor's degree in broadcast journalism and holds a master's degree in journalism from Ohio University (1985). While at Ohio, he produced a nightly student-led newscast on WOUB-TV in Athens. Bartlett has won more than a dozen Associated Press awards for reporting and four regional Emmys for reporting and writing. He is the author of *The Boy Who Delivered Joy* (2019), a true story about an extraordinary young cancer patient he met while on the job. Bartlett has taught broadcast writing classes as an adjunct professor at University of Kentucky and Florida A&M University.